Left column clippings

FUNERAL REQUISITES OF EVERY DESCRIPTION.

WALLER,
49 AND 50 DENZILLE STREET
(Merrion square).
Telephone No. 131.

SWITZER AND CO. LTD.

ANNUAL MEETING OF SHAREHOLDERS.

Yesterday the twenty-fifth annual meeting of the shareholders in Switzer and Co., Ltd., was held at the registered offices, 92 Grafton street, Dublin, for the purpose of receiving the directors' report and statement of accounts to the 31st January, 1915, and to declare dividends, to elect two directors and auditors for the ensuing year.

Mr. J. Gibson Moore, J.P., presided, and the other directors present were Messrs. John S. Switzer, James Clements, Fred. B. Switzer, and Charles I. Moore.

The directors' report stated—The profit after payment of all expenses amounts to £6,905 19s. 8d.; to this sum has to be added the amount brought forward from last year's accounts, £5,243 19s. 10d., making a total of £12,149 19s. 6d., out of which the following have been paid—Interest on Debenture Stock to 31st January, 1915, £2,000; interim dividend on the preference shares at the rate of 6 per cent. per annum, to 31st July, 1914, £750; interim dividend on the ordinary shares at the rate of 8 per cent. per annum to 31st July, 1914, £1,400—£4,150, leaving a sum of £7,999 19s. 6d. The directors recommend that this be applied as follows:—Final dividend on the preference shares at the rate of 6 per cent. per annum to 31st January, 1915, £750; dividend on the ordinary shares at the rate of 6 per cent. per annum to 31st January, (free of tax), making 7 per cent. for the year, £1,163 14s.; write off premises and fixtures account, £1,000; carry forward to next account, £5,086 5s. 6d.—£7,999 19s. 6d. trade for the months of August and September was seriously affected by the war, but the following four months business has improved considerably. The directors have placed to the credit of a premium reserve account a premium of £2 10s. per share on 758 new shares, which were issued last July to shareholders.

The Chairman, moving the adoption of the report and statement of accounts, said that the war affected every branch of commerce in Ireland. In a house like this, carrying on a high-class business amongst thousands of people, it would not be expected that they should wholly escape. The first half of the year was most satisfactory, but in the month of August there was a great falling off in receipts. Their best customers were evidently hard hit, and all classes of the community appeared to have purchased with caution. The directors took immediate steps to cope with the unprecedented situation. They were fortunate enough to secure some Government contracts, and by the most careful attention to the business of the house the sales gradually increased and expenses, as far as possible, were reduced. The buyers who had purchased for the house reported all the stock to be in good condition, and the purchasing public could rest assured that they would receive the same attention and get as good value at Switzer's now as in the years gone by, (Hear, hear.) He trusted that peace would soon be restored, and with that great blessing trade would revive in the city. (Hear, hear.) The directors had made every arrangement for and offered every encouragement to the members of the staff to join the King's Colours. (Applause.) They guaranteed to keep their various positions open for them on their return, and to pay half salaries while on active service, and in addition adequate financial provision was made for the dependents of three employés who as married men were called up as reservists. (Hear, hear.) He was sure the shareholders would approve of the action of the directors in that respect. (Applause.) During the past year No. 87 Grafton street came into the market. It adjoined their establishment, and the Board secured it believing it would prove a profitable investment for the company. (Hear, hear.) There was one item of ever-growing expense affecting them largely to which he would like to allude, and this was the taxation of the city. Individual merchants had no control over this, unless indeed that the ratepayers generally aroused themselves, and grappled with what was undoubtedly a menace to the prosperity and trade of Dublin. (Applause.) In conclusion, he desired to place on record the appreciation of the Board of the continued loyal services of the staff and the willing manner in which they assisted in making the business a success; and the directors believed that a courteous body of officials...

Right page (handwritten minutes)

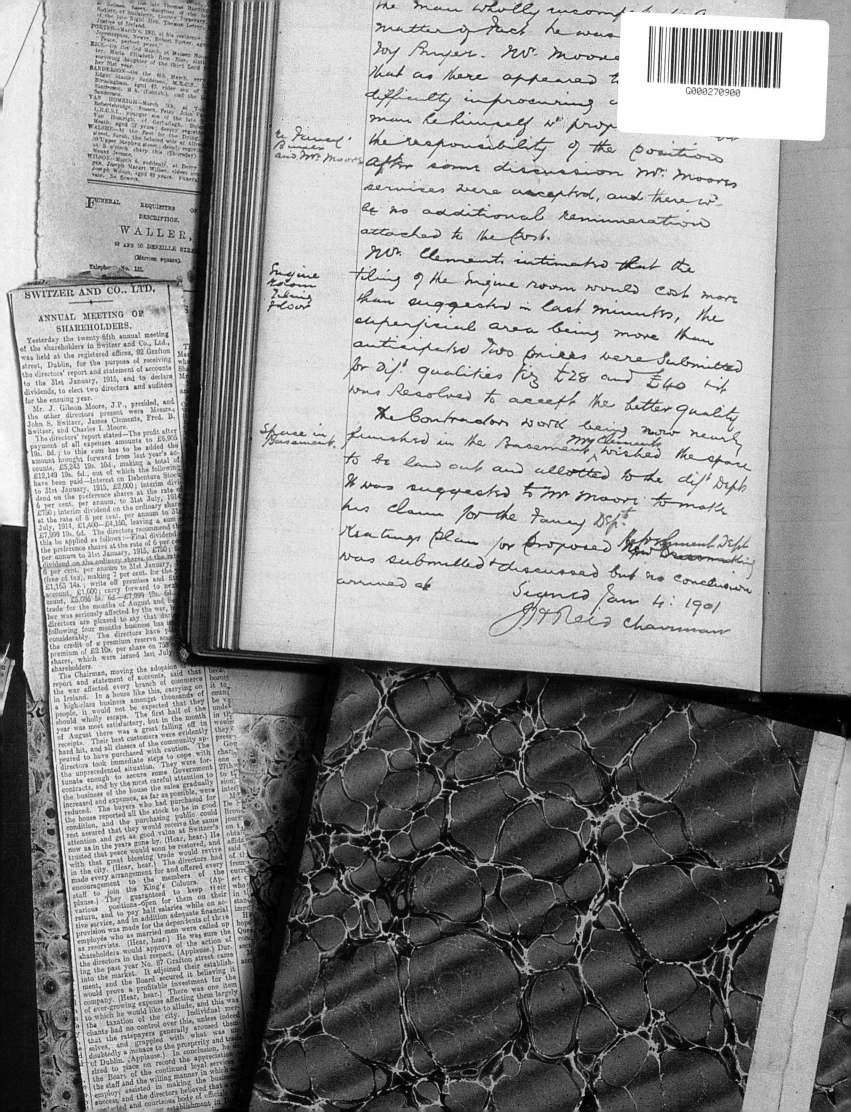

...the man wholly uncomfortable... matter of fact he was... boy buyer. Mr Moore... that as there appeared to... difficulty in procuring a... man he himself w' prop... the responsibility of the position after some discussion Mr Moore's services were accepted, and there w' be no additional remuneration attached to the post.

(margin: Mr Moore and Mr Moore's)

Mr Clements intimated that the tiling of the engine room would cost more than suggested in last minutes, the superficial area being more than anticipated. Two prices were submitted for dif' qualities viz £28 and £40. It was Resolved to accept the better quality.

(margin: Engine Room Tiling floor)

The Contractors work being now nearly finished in the Basement, Mr Clements wished the space to be laid out and allotted to the dif' Dep' It was suggested to Mr Moore to make his claim for the fancy Dep' Keating's plan for proposed New Dressmaking Dep' was submitted & discussed but no conclusion arrived at.

(margin: Space in Basement.)

Signed Jan 4: 1901
J H Reid chairman

Elegant Times

A Dublin Story

by

Anne Haverty

SONAS

© National Cartoon Company of Ireland Ltd.1995

First published by SONAS in 1995
Produced by National Cartoon Company of Ireland Ltd.
Written by Anne Haverty
Researched by Claire Graham
Based on an original idea by Brian MacDonald and Des Brown
and developed in association with them.
Designed by Josip Lizatovic
Compiled by Gráinne O'Rourke and Dudley Stewart
Illustrations by Josip Lizatovic

Additional Illustrations: Steve Simpson and Roger Horgan
Computer Graphics by: John Hussey assisted by Mark Smullen and Oisín McGann
Editor: George McCullagh

Colour Separations by Dublin Online Typographic Services Ltd. (DOTS)
Printed and bound in Ireland by ColourBooks Ltd.

ISBN : 1-899565-01-9

British Library Cataloguing in Publication Data.
A Catalogue record for this book is available from the British Library.

PHOTOGRAPHIC ACKNOWLEDGMENTS

Page 4&5 Wedding Dress and Veil courtesy of Brides International, From "Lady of the House"; *Page 6* Dublin and old T.C.D., *Page 10* St. Stephen's Green and Leinster House, *Page 11* Carlisle Bridge and College Green, *Page 13* College Green, Sackville St. and Provost House, *Page 26* Grafton St. and Toilet mask, *Page 31* Vice Regal Lodge Room, *Page 36* Typical Victorian dress, *Page 38* Ladies in costumes, *Page 40* COCO Ad and Lady, *Page 42* Jewellery, *Page 59* Dublin at war, *Page 74* Kennedys Bread Ad, *Page 14* Cork Hill – Picturesque Dublin Old and New 1891, *Page 24* Brown Thomas, a private collection, *Page 25* Grafton St. c. 1865, a private collection, *Page 46* Drapers' Assistant from Mandate Union, *Page 51* Original Scroll provided by Bob Fitzgerald, *Page 54* Brown Family, a private collection, *Page 60* War Poster from Trinity History Workshop as published in Ireland and the First World War, *Page 63* Eno's Fruit Salt, "Memoirs" A pictorial celebration for Dublin's millenium, Jefferson Smurfit Group plc, From "The Cashman Collection"; *Page 67* Michael Collins, Four Courts, *Page 67* Artillery from "The life and times of Eamonn de Valera Gill & Macmillan, *Page 74* Juvenile Mannequins, 1930s Irish Press (28.10.33), *Page 75* Dublin's Prettiest Girl from Dublin's Evening Mail (31.10.33), *Page 75* Pat Rooney, Irish Independent (3.11.33), *Page 108* Galen Weston, Tony Hauser, *Page 109* Shopfront, a Brown Thomas postcard, *Page 110* Norah McGuinness, "Creation Scene", *Page 111* 3-D relief by Brendan Pierce, *Page 114* Jimmy Duffy, a private collection, Courtesy of Susan Kennedy; *Page 115* George McCullagh, *Page 116* Paul Kelly, *Page 116* Deirdre Kelly, *Page 117* Hilary Weston, *Page 119* Crane Bucket.

SPECIAL THANKS TO:

Tommy Beatty, Nita Boylan, Úna Brady, Ita Brazil, Alan Brown, Sylvia Byrne (née Herron), Michael Cahill, Donough Callaghan, Mary Campbell, Gertrude Clarke, Barbara Corballis, John Costelloe, Catríona Crowe, Edna Deacon, Dublin Public Library, Frances Duff, Grace Duncan, Brian Farrell, Bob FitzGerald, Wally and Pauline Garland, Gilbert Library Pearse Street, Margaret Hamilton-Reid, Sean Kenna, Terry Keogh, Paul Kelly, Vincent Poklewski Koziell, Frances McAnespie, Máire Mac An tSaoí, George McCullagh, Therese McEntee, James McGuire, Rhoda McGuinness, Cecily McMenamin, National Archives, National Library, Mick O'Keefe, Colleen O'Neill, Jenny O'Neill, Peggy O'Neill, Jimmy O'Raw, Harry Osman, Stephen Palmer, Peter Prentice, John Redmond, Dick Roche, Fiona Roche, R.I.A.I., Marie Scott, Mary Smullen, James Switzer, John Taylor, Gerry Walker, Larry Yourell.

Dedication

People create great stores, great streets
and great cities.
We dedicate this book to the people who
lived, visited, shopped and served in Brown
Thomas and Switzers, Grafton Street
and Dublin and to those who will
continue to do so.

In the rush of modern living, it is seldom that we are given an opportunity to reflect on Ireland's changing social history and the anecdotes of past times.

It is the intention of this book to assist in such reflection and to reveal the vision and foresight of those families who, over the years, have nurtured and developed the trading activities of two great shopping venues, Switzers and Brown Thomas. Very significant decisions affecting their fortunes were made in the beginning by the Switzer, the Brown and the Thomas families. These families were succeeded in ownership and dedicated leadership by the Hamilton Reids and the Moores, and on the other side of the street the Selfridges, the Purcells and the McGuires. All contributed to the enjoyment and employment of the citizens of Dublin and the wider Ireland.

The vision which Galen and Hilary Weston displayed in becoming involved in Brown Thomas twenty five years ago and Switzers twenty years later is now clearly seen.

The events which have brought us thus far result from their great personal commitment to Ireland, to Dublin and to trading of the highest quality.

It has been my pleasure and that of many others to have been part of these events, and we leave it now to those further removed than us to recount the achievements of these times.

Under continuing Weston ownership, the future looks even brighter and even more interesting than the past.

Dublin,
February 1995.

George McCullagh,
Editor

On a morning in February 1995, as the new primrose facade of the former Switzers glowed in the pale spring light outside, Hilary Weston cut the ceremonial tape and declared the reborn Brown Thomas of Grafton Street open. The new Brown Thomas was directly across the street from the old establishment and the move symbolised the marriage of two of Dublin's greatest and most venerable retail businesses.

Among those present were some of the oldest friends and associates of both businesses as well as some of the youngest and most recent. The night before, more than a thousand invited guests had celebrated the opening at one of Dublin's most glamorous parties of the year.

But in a sense all of Dublin participated in the ceremony, for generations of Dubliners had known and loved these shops and had waited with some excitement for the opening of the new premises. Both shops had been associated with the happiest moments of their lives - weddings, birthdays, Christmas celebrations… the choosing of a hat for the Horse Show, a tweed jacket for walks in the west, a bikini for a holiday in the sun, the first three-piece suite for an engaged couple, a special present for a special friend…

This morning, Grafton Street was crowded as it had been now for almost two centuries. By the early 1990s, 20,000 people were estimated to pass along it every hour. Today, no matter how hurried they were, few could resist entering the splendid glass doors set in mellow Portland stone to appraise the new shop.

As they passed under the crimson awnings and the classically-styled Brown Thomas lettering on the facade, a clean, muted elegance met them everywhere. A curving limestone staircase, evocative of the great houses of Ireland and of an opulent period in the history of Switzers itself, top-lit and carpeted in red, rose through three floors.

Faithful customers of Brown Thomas were pleased to see the famous chandeliers re-installed in the new premises. They would also have noted with pleasure that the Victorian couches and chairs which had eased the process of choosing clothes and shoes in the old shop stood about comfortably in the new. Their purchases came in wrappings that incorporated the traditional black and white of Brown Thomas, the Switzers' stripes and a paean to Grafton Street by poet Patrick Kavanagh. The shop expressed an elegant blend of tradition and modernity, both Irish and international.

Dublin has always been proud of its long and colourful past. More than any of the city's historic thoroughfares, Grafton Street represents the old times and the old ways. For the best part of three hundred years it has been a place of resort for strollers and shoppers, the heart of Dublin society.

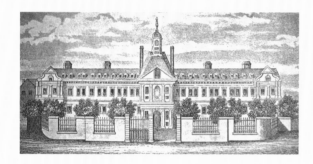

Dublin, at the end of the twentieth century, is a modern bustling city of over a million inhabitants. In the 1600s, it was a small and irregular town of timber and plaster structures clustered around the fortress of Dublin Castle. To the west it reached St. James's Gate; to the south only as far as the Coombe. A medieval church stood at almost every corner, dominated by the two Cathedrals, Christchurch and St. Patrick's.

In the open space to the east by the river sat rosy-hued Tudoresque Trinity College - yet to acquire its grand Palladian facade. The College looked up towards the Castle and between them lay Hoggen Green, where rooting swine were a nuisance to students on their way to the inns and taverns of the town. From Hoggen Green, a bucolic but often unpassable cow-path known as Span Lane wound its way up to another green, St. Stephen's, a patch of commonage lately declared a public park but infamous for the footpads and other insalubrious characters who lurked there after dark.

Top: *Panoramic view of old Dublin.*
Above: *Trinity College, early 17th Century.*
Below: *When the Palladian facade was added, Trinity assumed the shape familiar to Dubliners today.*

WEST FRONT OF THE COLLEGE

Inhabitants of the town were mainly English-speaking and loyal to the Crown, descended variously from Danish, Norman and more recent settlements.

The native population, in a turbulent century of rebellion, religious reformation, and foreign wars, had at many junctures proved themselves hostile to the city's settled inhabitants and had been for a long time excluded from its centre. As everyday normality began to prevail, they congregated in villages outside its walls.

Dublin was already assuming the character of the capital of the King's Irish realm, with a mixed population, more relaxed about their security and with growing ambitions to become citizens of a suitably grand and urbane city.

Commercial activity was concentrated in the narrow streets and alleys around the Castle and City Hall, known then as the Tholsel. Skinner's Row (now Christchurch Place) was where the tanners and leather-workers traditionally had their shops; traders in Fishamble Street dealt in fish, and in Wine Tavern Street alehouses and inns were open for business at all hours of the day and night. Above their doors swung picturesque painted signs to denote their trade to customers unable to read. Dublin's first newspaper, the *Dublin Newsletter*, was printed in 1685 at the sign of the Leather Bottle in Skinner's Row. It was a single sheet containing one article of news and two advertisements.

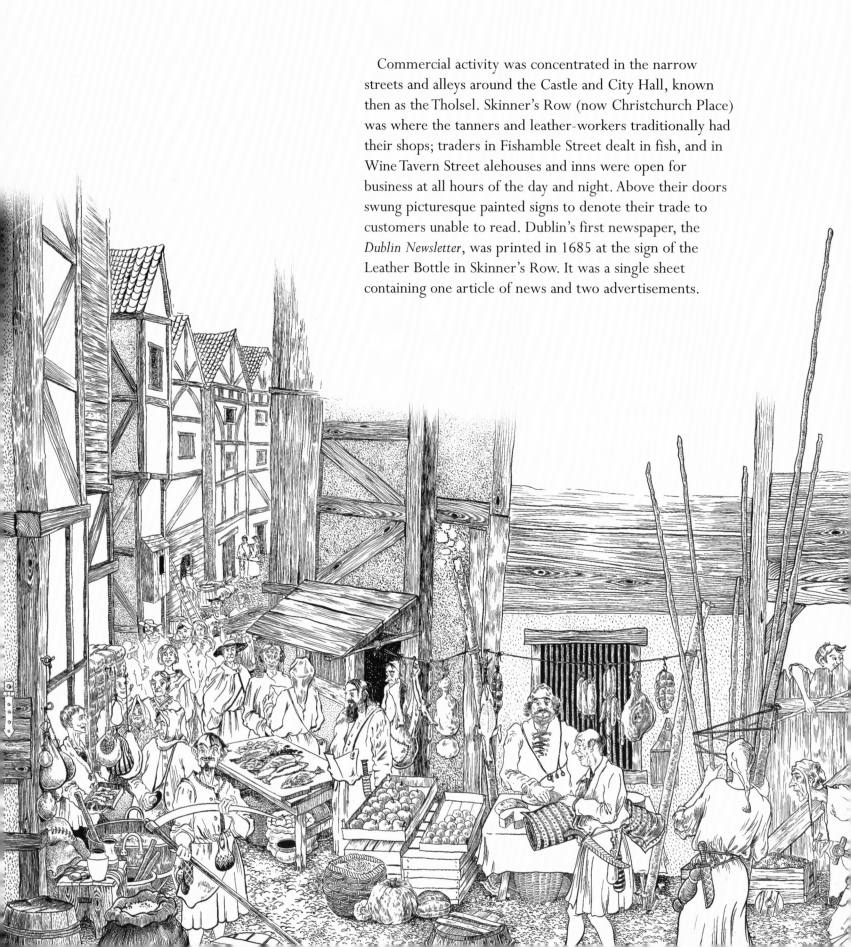

With the Restoration of Charles II in the mid-century and the appointment of James Butler, Duke of Ormonde to govern Ireland as its first Viceroy, Dublin's expansion to the north and south began. Ormonde, returned from a long exile in France, was a sophisticated grandee who with determination and zest set about constructing a city worthy to compete with Paris in beauty and splendour. The Royal Hospital, the creation of the Phoenix Park as a deer park for the people's enjoyment, the line of open quays by the river in the Parisian style were all due to Ormonde. He was recalled to London in 1688 but he had established a trend that the Corporation carried on after his departure with confidence and panache.

St. Stephen's Green was enclosed to form a municipal square, larger than any in London, with fine terraces of houses around it. Country gentlemen, who finally had unquestioned tenure of their lands and rents, sat in the new Parliament House on College Green. Eager to participate in the pomp and conviviality of the season, they needed townhouses to accommodate themselves and their families. With them came a tide of men of the professional class such as engineers, lawyers, civil servants and doctors.

The expansion first was northwards across the river. Henrietta Street, with its severely fine Georgian-style mansions, was the fashionable place to live. The vast and airy mall of Sackville Street was another. Then in 1745 the young Earl of Kildare broke rank and, on the wrong side of the river, built a magnificent Italianate residence off Coote Lane, renaming it Kildare Street. This is now Leinster House. Asked why he had chosen such a remote and unfashionable spot, Kildare is rumoured to have replied: "They will follow me wherever I go". And they did.

Top: *Stephen's Green, Dublin.*
Bottom: *Leinster House in
The Earl of Kildare's day.*

The environs of the College, centre of learning and prestige, could not remain isolated for long and soon fine brick residences with spacious rooms and orchards and stable lanes at their backs were colonising rustic Span Lane. Worthy now of a more glorious name, the new street was called Grafton Street in honour of young Henry Fitzroy, Duke of Grafton, natural son of Charles II but also a hero who fought with King William in the Williamite Wars. As a homage to the monarch "held in pious and immortal memory", the name reflected the city's firmly loyal identity as King William's Irish capital.

It was however the opening of Carlisle Bridge in 1792 (now O'Connell Bridge) adjacent to the rejuvenated Temple Bar area of Dublin that sounded the death-knell for the north side. The rigged trading-schooners now lay down-river behind the new bridge. And, steep and narrow though it was, it joined the thoroughfare of Sackville Street to flourishing Grafton Street and beyond, marooned Henrietta Street and gradually marginalised the ancient section of the town.

Above: *Old Carlisle Bridge, Dublin.*
Left: *18th Century College Green.*

The houses of Grafton Street assumed the grandeur that had belonged to Henrietta Street and residents could boast that gentry such as Lords Kinsale, Dunsany and Newhaven kept townhouses here. However, since nobility moved on when trade moved in, the nexus of commercial life remained for a long time where it had always been. Business was not entirely absent from the street - in the 1750s Samuel Whyte was running his famous academy for young gentlemen at no. 75 - but to do their shopping the ladies of Grafton Street travelled up Dame Street in their private sedan-chairs to the thriving manufacturing area around the Castle now known as the Liberties.

Right: *Lady in a quilted petticoat, c. 1745*

The new prosperity of the Liberties was due largely to the influx of Huguenot refugees from France who brought the weaving trade with them. Irish weavers with whom the Huguenots shared their secret arts were soon famous abroad for their manufacture of brocades, delicate paduasoys, silks, linen and poplin. The Coombe sang with the hum of hundreds of looms.

Conveyed there by sedan-chair, met by local women ready to be hired as porters of her purchases, and greeted by the proprietor at the door of his shop known by the painted sign it traded under, an elegant lady with money in her purse could pass a pleasant afternoon in the Liberties.

At the Blackamoor's Head in Francis Street, she could examine black calicos and russets for petticoats, shoes at the sign of the Cock in High Street and stays in the Coombe at the Spread Eagle. At the Royal Stocking in Nicholas Street, she no doubt browsed through their stock of "all sorts of figured and plain silk stockings, French mill'd caps, and silk mitts for ladies". In a more prosaic mood, she could buy bellows for the fire at the Cheshire Cheese in Bride's Alley, coal at The Three Cats on Aston's Quay and coffee and cocoa at the Parrot in Plunkett Street.

Mass-production of fabric began in 1815 when Cartwright invented the power weaving-loom. The hum of the hand-loom died away and the Liberties, though it continued to teem with life, became a place of poverty and desolation.

Meanwhile, those with an eye to profitable commerce were alighting on Grafton Street, central and easily accessible to the residents of the grand squares and gracious streets that were stretching outward east and south of the growing city. Businesses and shops of the more genteel sort were opening up. As they did, the occupants of houses on Grafton Street moved on to more strictly residential areas. Grafton Street was on its way. By the end of the century, it would be known as the Bond Street of Dublin.

Top: *College Green in the early 1800s.*
Middle*: Sackville Street (Now O'Connell Street) in 1756.*
Bottom*: The Provost's House, Trinity College.*

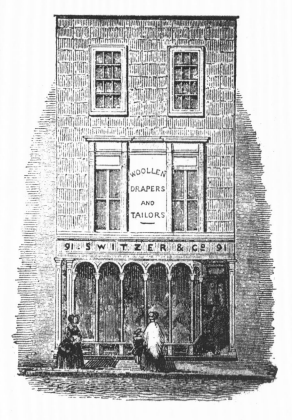

A young man of German extraction called John Wright Switzer was among these enterprising businessmen. Born in Newpark, Co. Tipperary in 1806, Switzer belonged to the Palatine community, refugees who had fled from their Rhineland homes in the Palatinate a century before because of religious persecution. The Palatines were Lutheran and, like the Huguenots, were skilled craftsmen. Some settled in Limerick, others in Dublin.

John Wright Switzer's branch of the family, originally from the German town of Assenheim, had settled in Tipperary. His father, Christopher, was a younger son and one of eleven children. John grew up in relative poverty on a small farm of eight acres. Seeing little future in farming, he set out for Dublin to seek his fortune.

He began his business life peddling suit lengths from a barrow around the bustling alleys of the Liberties and was clearly successful because in 1832 at the age of twenty-three he had progressed to trading as a Military Tailor and Draper out of an establishment on Cork Hill. In 1838, he transferred his business to 91 Grafton Street, a much more prestigious situation, calling his new shop a Woollen Drapers.

This was the term used for a shop selling clothing for men. At street level, customers were ushered into the opulent oil-lit dimness inside, to choose from the display of fine cloths. Upstairs were the workrooms where tailors and seamstresses made the cloth into garments. Among the seamstresses in 1840 was Isobel Fowler, who made hand-sewn waistcoats and was the great-grandmother of the poet Richard Murphy. No. 91 also housed Mrs Diana Nolan's baby linen warehouse.

Top: *The start of it all, 91 Grafton Street.*
John Wright Switzer's first shop.
Bottom: *Guests arrive at a Dublin Castle levee.*
Right: *Humble beginnings in the Liberties of the 19th Century.*

By 1838 when John Switzer arrived, Grafton Street, described as "half a wheatfield" only forty years before, had assumed the shape we know today and was lined with commercial activities of the kind that catered for luxury tastes - milliners, jewellers, booksellers, cigar-divans and confectioners. The stable-lanes had been named Duke Lane (the upper half of which was later to become Anne's Lane) and the orchards had given way to brick and stone.

Next door to Switzers at no. 90 was William Mansfield, dressing-case maker and fancy repository. On the other side at no. 92 was Boardmans: a shirtmaker, hosier, glover and military outfitter. A shop's proudest boast was that it was official supplier to the Lord Lieutenant or even, but more rarely, His Majesty. As early as the 1840s, Sarah Mitchell, Confectioner, at no. 10 could claim to enjoy the patronage of both.

John Switzer had a reputation for kindness and fair dealing but he was also ambitious. Businesses came and went in Grafton Street but Switzers thrived. By the 1850s, Diana Nolan's baby linen had moved to no. 93 where she shared the shop with Hazeltons, shirtmaker and military outfitter; while John Switzer remained in sole possession of no. 91, having formed a company with John Beatty of 43 Wicklow Street.

Bottom: *Grafton Street in 1838 Switzers and some of its earliest competitors.*

He was married by now, to Lucinda Walker, had two children, Bamlet and Julia, and had bought Moyvalley House in Co. Kildare, originally built as a hotel for passengers on the Royal Canal. This was where he now lived, reflecting a new trend among well-to-do shopkeepers to no longer live over the shop but to take a prestigious house remote from their place of trading. Spas were fashionable at the time and Switzer, with his German background, had an interest in hydropathic medicine. Shortly after acquiring Moyvalley House, he opened a medico-hydropathic institute there.

Switzer was enabled to come up to town daily from Kildare to oversee his flourishing business by the revolutionary new transport system, the railway, which brought him to Kingsbridge Station. From here, he could take either a Dublin growler or a side-car to Grafton Street. But being a health fiend, he would often prefer the brisk walk along the Quays and through Dame Street and College Green to his place of business.

Below: *The pleasant scene of the Royal Canal near the home of John Wright Switzer.*

In 1848, almost directly across the street at no. 16, an equally ambitious and go-getting young man bought out the millinery and dress showrooms of Underwood and Co. and opened a haberdashery shop. This was Hugh Brown, a buyer at Todd, Burns in Mary Street. His wife was Marianne Ward Riddle, a descendant of the first Surveyor General of Ireland, Sir Robert Ward.

A cameo portrait of Hugh Brown shows a lean, intelligent-looking man with a determined jutting chin and the upright gravitas of the Victorian gentleman. His wife, in her streamered bonnet, looks equally practical and effective though suitably demure and correct.

In the following year, 1849, Hugh Brown joined forces with a friend, James Thomas, also a buyer at Todd, Burns. Together they bought out Mary Hayd'n, milliner and court dressmaker next door at no. 17 and began trading as a general draper and haberdasher. This was where "the lunatic angel", the radical young poet Percy Bysshe Shelley lodged on his second visit to Ireland in 1812 and no. 17 was christened the Cave of Abdullah by the Dublin wits because of the wild-haired romantics who called on him there.

Bottom: *Grafton Street in 1849 on the arrival of Brown, Thomas and Co.*
Opposite: *Brown, Thomas and Co. expands and develops its characteristically grand façade.*

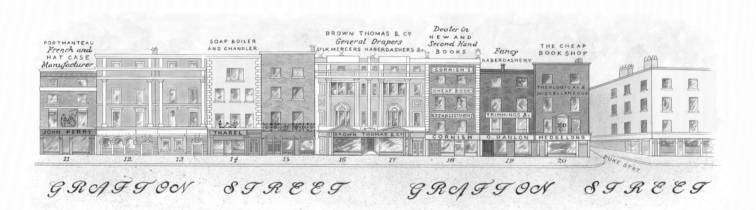

A few years later, Brown and Thomas expanded their
business again, taking over no. 15. This was the premises of
John Maccaud, Gymnastic Academy and Anthony Dillon,
artists' colour man and map seller. Brown, Thomas and Co.,
15-17 Grafton Street, was now solidly established.

Hugh Brown and James Thomas established their new shop at one of the most troubled times in Irish history. The Great Famine was still running its terrible course. Rural devastation was impelling hordes of the starving and plague-stricken towards the city, so that its population swelled. There was almost a full-scale revolt in Dublin in 1848, inspired by the Young Irelanders, and the streets were filled with "red jackets varied by blue uniforms of the artillery and light cavalry". Even good houses in Grafton Street, wrote *The Evening Mail*, were dirty and dilapidated, the windows patched, the shops closed and papered with auction notices and notices from the Poor Law Commissioners and the Insolvent Court.

But Brown and Thomas were optimistic and probably astute speculators and they were proved right. Paradoxically, the aftermath of the Famine was a prosperous time for Ireland. Holdings were being consolidated, a new type of grazier farmer was emerging and tenants were more prompt and regular with their rents. All over Ireland the new prosperity was felt in the towns and the capital city was no exception. There was more money about and an increasing demand for goods to spend it on.

It was about this time that Veblen identified the new phenomenon he called conspicuous consumption. Ostentation and appropriateness in dress for a whole new variety of purposes and social occasions were becoming imperative for the fashionable woman and man. The industrial revolution created a new type of consumer, the newly-rich manufacturer who revelled in his possessions and wealth and expected his wife and daughters to sumptuously display it in their dress and accoutrements.

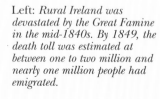

Left: *Rural Ireland was devastated by the Great Famine in the mid-1840s. By 1849, the death toll was estimated at between one to two million and nearly one million people had emigrated.*

In the 1830s, a girl had thought herself rich, "with one silk dress and a few muslins, all untrimmed, and one summer and winter bonnet a year... Many, whatever their rank, had less, and wore no ornaments on neck or arms until they married". In the 1880s, women – matrons and girls alike – were spending four times as much on clothes as they had some decades before.

The sheer quantity of material alone required for a voluminous bustled dress of the period with its enormous sleeves must have increased four-fold. In the heyday of the crinoline in the 1850s, it was not unknown for forty-eight yards of material to be used in a dress and there were also the ample petticoats often worn beneath it instead of the cumbersome cage. There were essential accessories; hats, collars, gloves, trimmings of all descriptions, muffs, fichus, furs, shawls, footwear, most of them required to be different for morning, afternoon or evening wear.

Victorian etiquette was strict, complex and pervasive. A woman had to possess an entire mourning costume, since she went into mourning dress for long periods on the demise of the most distant relation. Her dresses, jackets and mantles had to be black, also her petticoats – while her outer garments had to be covered or trimmed with crêpe. Her ornaments had to be jet, her handkerchiefs bordered in black, her parasol trimmed with crêpe. Widow's attire had its own set of rules, extending even to the length of the black streamers attached to their bonnets.

A New Safety Crinoline

Top: *The crinoline liberated Victorian women.*
Bottom: *New Shape Jacket, Price on Stand complete 12/6 each.*

In the mid-century too, women were getting out and about more. The nobility would occasionally join the rising middle class in using the public omnibuses instead of using their own private conveyances. Dublin's pavements were asphalted in the 1850s and though splendid carriages jostled for position along Grafton Street, strolling in the town had become respectable among the elegant of both sexes. The custom of taking a day out to shop began, and this included window-shopping. Displays were not yet artistic but the plenitude of goods arranged higgledy-piggledy behind the new plate glass windows were indicative of the ever-increasing variety the shops offered.

Queen Victoria, trekking about the Highlands of Scotland, made walking fashionable and this too necessitated a "Balmoral" costume, part of which was a pair of Balbriggan stockings. These were fine hand-sewn hose, originally made in Balbriggan in Co. Dublin but later the term was applied to any fine cotton stockings, wherever they were made.

Gentlemen too had a panoply of outfits for different occasions. And of course everyone, man, woman and even child, wore a hat outdoors at all times.

To supply all these burgeoning needs, indeed often to create them, and to guide and assist the anxious customer through the minefield of dress etiquette, there was the draper. The successful draper was enjoying a new status and power and, in tune with the times, he was expansionist and forward-looking. Typical of this new breed were Hugh Brown, James Thomas and John Switzer.

Above: *Hats could be bought
for all occasions.*
Opposite: *Comparing notes
on the best bargains.*

Immediately they acquired nos. 16 and 17, Brown and Thomas set about the improvement and enlargement of their premises. An up-and-coming young architect, William Caldbeck, was employed for a fee of £40 to prepare the plans. Brown and Thomas were acquainted with Caldbeck because he had also prepared plans for Todd, Burns and they knew him to be a competent, if not very innovative, architect. Caldbeck later designed bank houses throughout the provinces for the National Bank and his sturdy edifices still grace the main street of many a country town.

They commissioned the replacement of the Georgian facade with a modern Victorian one, alteration and removal of the Georgian interior and the construction of an extension to the rear. All this refurbishment paid off handsomely because their business boomed.

The Royal Dublin Society Great Exhibition was held on Leinster Lawn in 1853, showing the fruits of the revolution in industrial manufacture; agricultural implements, railway carriages and mechanisms, silk, velvet and tapestry, paper-hangings, glass and ceramics. Brown & Thomas were sufficiently established to present ornate cases displaying their wares. A few years later when no.15 had been acquired, the services of Caldbeck were called upon again.

Top: *Brown Thomas displays its wares at the Great Exhibition of 1853.*
Right: *Caldbeck's designs for the new store.*
Opposite: *A typical day on Grafton Street.*

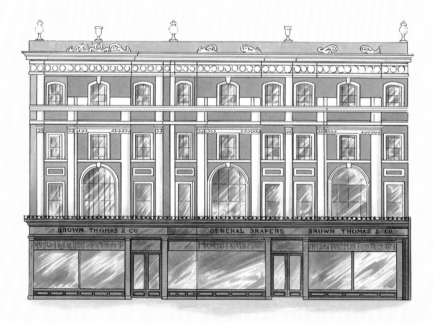

The new premises at no.15 had a substantial garden space at the back and Caldbeck embarked on an extensive extension and re-modelling to include this space as well as the building itself. The Georgian facade gave way to a heavily re-modelled one which matched the new front of nos. 16 and 17 and a new warehouse was built on the open yards at the back.

"Brown, Thomas and Co.", a contemporary journal noted in 1859, "have commenced another large extension to their premises and this expenditure will be upwards of £2,000". The builder was Mr Rooney and Mr Caldbeck received a fee of £20 for the warehouse design.

This enlarged and handsome shop was now styled Brown, Thomas, & Co., Silk Mercers, Linendrapers, Haberdashers and Milliners. Soon, both its owners moved to the new suburb of Rathgar: James Thomas to Mayfield and Hugh Brown to Highfield Road. With its red-brick villas and leafy gardens front and rear, Rathgar was regarded as one of the most prestigious and desirable places to live. Men of a practical inclination preferred it to the similar suburb of Pembroke (now Ballsbridge) because though Rathgar's services were not as good, its rates were lower.

Top: *Saturday morning shopping on Grafton Street.*
Above: *Suffering for fashion.*

In 1859 too, John Switzer and his partner William Beatty, now trading as The Commercial Hall Co., were refurbishing and extending their premises, perhaps in a healthy spirit of competition with their rivals across the street. They acquired number 92 and architects were invited to submit designs for the new frontages on Grafton Street and Wicklow Street. Four architectural firms competed - Messrs Geoghegan, Rawson Carroll, Carmichael and Jones and Ferguson.

Rawson Carroll's Italianate design was the winner, partly because it was considered that his plans could be carried out for a lower sum than any of the others. The Commercial Hall Co. started a trend, for which architects were grateful, by paying £10 each to the also-rans to compensate them for the expense of competing.

Switzers also acquired land from the Church of the Discalced Carmelites in Clarendon Street during this period. The Church had two laneways leading from its site off Grafton Street (a throw-back to Penal Times when Catholic churches could not front onto a main street). Because these laneways had become too popular with courting couples for the church's taste, it was happy to sell the laneway leading to Wicklow Street to Switzers, who incorporated it into its expansion plans.

By 1862, Brown Thomas had acquired number 6, Duke Street. *The Irish Builder*, discussing the blockages caused on Grafton Street by the heavy traffic of carriages, noted that the problem was somewhat alleviated by the new side entrances to Switzers and Brown Thomas on Wicklow Street and Duke Street.

James Thomas however did not long enjoy the renovations and expansion at his new premises. He died at home in Mayfield on June 27th 1867, leaving a fortune of £23,000 to his widow, Margaret. Control of the business passed into Hugh Brown's hands, who continued to trade as Brown, Thomas & Co., because of the glowing and far-reaching reputation the shop had earned under that name. He continued the steady colonisation of Duke Street. In 1874, he leased No. 5.

John Switzer continued to flourish. In 1886, now aged eighty, he acquired neighbouring shops, no. 88 from Adolphe Chargeois, Watchmaker and Jeweller, and no. 88a from Crichton's Family and General Mourning Warehouse.

In 1890, when his partner William Beatty too was dead, John Switzer formed a public company, with himself as its first chairman. He was 84 years old. Having discarded the name, The Commercial Hall Co., and reverted proudly to its first soubriquet, Switzer & Co. was now a vast emporium of the most elegant and quality goods, stretching for almost a block down Grafton Street and around the corner into a good portion of Wicklow Street.

Directors on the Board of Switzer & Co. included John Gibson Moore of Llandaff Hall, Merrion and John Hamilton Reid of Lisnoe, Rathmines. John Gibson Moore was a merchant, John Hamilton Reid a banker who was bored with banking. For the next eighty years, a Switzer, a Moore or a Hamilton Reid would be Chairman of Switzer's Board. It was a tight-knit harmonious partnership, the Switzers bringing artistry and finesse, the Moores good merchandizing and the Hamilton Reids financial control.

In the following year, on the 22nd of December 1891, John Wright Switzer died at the age of eighty-five at Moyvalley House. The one-time pedlar left over £20,000.

His competitor, Hugh Brown, had died almost a decade before, on the 4th of March 1882, also at home in Highfield Road. His fortune was considerably greater. He left the sum of £116,000 to his wife, Marianne.

By the 1890s when a great future had been ensured for the shops they had created on Grafton Street, their founders were dead. But they left behind a legacy that their heirs would consolidate. The heyday of the department store was at hand.

Top: *Victorian ladies taking the air.*
Right: *The Switzer expansion continues.*

Shops were no longer dark mahogany dominated premises where stuffs and silks glowed in the oil-lit gloom and the proprietor invited his customers into the back parlour to complete their transactions. Electrification arrived in Dublin in the 1880s and the up-to-date establishments immediately installed the magical new method of lighting that could show their goods to the best advantage. The number of assistants employed was growing, hierarchies among them were being established and in shops like Brown, Thomas and Switzers, jobs with new titles were being instituted.

A customer was greeted at the grand entrance by a commissionaire, and welcomed, usually by name since loyal patronage of a particular shop was customary, by a shop-walker. The walkers with their graciousness and style gave tone to an establishment, though the timid often found them snooty and intimidating. Their role was to ascertain what the customer was in search of, lead her to one of the plush chairs lined up by the counter with its tempting and scented array and seat her while an assistant was imperiously summoned to serve her.

Top: *Boot stand, 19th Century.*
Right: *A commissionaire gracefully greets a customer.*
Opposite: *Customers now had a far greater array from which to choose.*

When she had made her purchases, she was led to a porter who parcelled them; and then perhaps to a delivery boy who carried the parcels to her carriage. As she went out, a walker stepped forward to open the door for her and the commissionaire gave her a gracious bow. It was the age of the servant when labour could be bought cheaply and excellence in service was regarded as the key to good business.

As for the customers of the time, Brown Thomas's prestige depended largely on its aristocratic patronage but of course as a thriving department store it included among its customers not only members of the professional classes but of the mercantile and business classes as well, among them the rising Catholic middle-classes. Prominent among those who patronised Brown, Thomas and Switzers were of course the ladies who needed a constant supply of gowns, hats and all the accessories that went with them for their round of social engagements, many of them at Dublin Castle or at the Viceregal Lodge in Phoenix Park.

To be on the Viceregal list, especially during the "season", which took place in the late winter, was the highest mark of distinction for Dublin inhabitants. The Viceregal Court was the hub of the social life of the capital. And it was not, unlike St. James's Court in London, exclusively aristocratic. Landed families were on the list but so were professional and army families. Dublin was heavily garrisoned at this time and there was a constant coming and going of the families of officers, and a lot of girls eager to meet a handsome aide-de-camp. There was a round of levees, balls, drawing room receptions and garden-parties, centred around the Castle and there were also private affairs in grand houses. All these demanded a brisk turnover in gowns.

There was another stratum of Dublin Society, those who were not on the Viceregal list but were on the list held at the Mansion House. Habituees of the Mansion House, home of the Corporation, were likely to be sympathetic with the wave of nationalism and republicanism beginning to sweep the country and to shun the Castle. Few were on both lists. But those who went to the Mansion House wanted finery too.

Top: *The latest fashions are displayed at the Dublin Horse Show, 1908.*
Bottom: *The Viceregal lodge where the gentry flaunted their style.*
Opposite: *Her purchases made, a customer is shown to her carriage.*

Then there were families who came up from the country for the season and annual events like the Horse Show. It was a long-established custom for a country family to take a suite at the Shelbourne Hotel on St. Stephen's Green during their stays in Dublin, giving rise to a constant passage of delivery boys from Grafton Street, their arms piled high with parcels and hat-boxes.

Brown, Thomas & Co. at this time was described in a contemporary article as "enormous in extent", and enjoying "the largest share of patronage probably bestowed on any house in the city... drawn from the most aristocratic and wealthy circles in society".

What was especially commendable and admirable however
was their stock of Irish linens and lace and their ingenious
practice of making up the latest designs in gowns from the
Parisian models in Irish manufactured materials. People
were constantly urged to "buy Irish" in these years but the
fashionable had an unpatriotic hankering for the newest Paris
fashion mode.

To solve this problem, buyers, on their return from Paris
with the latest novelties and styles, handed them over for
copying to the skilled staff of seamstresses in the workrooms
upstairs. Though there was doubtless a strong element of
patriotism in Brown Thomas's devotion to Irish goods, it was
also astute on their part as it was a shop that the Mansion
House set could patronise with an easy conscience.

In the busy season, as many as 250 needlewomen and cutters were employed in Brown Thomas workrooms. On the floor, there was a growing army of assistants, of whom a small but steadily increasing number were women. Another of Brown Thomas's strengths was its well-established business of exporting goods to America, Australia and India. This was known as the colonial trade and the company's taste in goods and efficiency in sending them were so renowned that no foreigner, it was said, "wishing to bring away some memento of his visit - generally a specimen of Irish work at its best - leaves the city without paying the celebrated house in Grafton Street a visit". Another army of parcellers, post-boys and porters was employed to satisfy this substantial section of their clientele residing in far-flung places.

The number of employees in Brown Thomas's various departments had reached 300 at the end of the century.

Switzers had a staff of 250, many of them living in the staff quarters at the top of the house above their respective shops. This was a universal practice among shops from the largest to the smallest. It began as a means of guarding the safety and good morals of the assistant, generally a young person who might be away from home for the first time and for whom the accommodation available in the city in the form of digs or lodgings was thought to present perils.

Of course it was a also a means of economising on their housing costs and in most cases on their keep. Living in, they required only pocket-money, usually very minimal. For large shops like Switzers and Brown Thomas, it also required the employment of another set of workers in the regions above-stairs to look after them, from the Staff Superintendents to the cooks and domestic servants.

At the turn of the century, 69 people lived over Brown, Thomas at nos. 15-17. Assistants, office clerks and domestic servants, they came from almost every county in Ireland, Kerry to Cavan; of every religion, from Congregationalist to Catholic, though there was a preponderance of Church of Ireland; and ranging from sixteen year old apprentices to 56 year old Thomas White, House Steward who supervised them all. Most of them were men - there were only seven women Drapers' Assistants.   Of the 69, not one of them was married, a fact remarkably prevalent among drapers' assistants generally.

Above Switzers, 78 people lived in the attic rooms at no. 92. As a group they closely resembled Brown Thomas; of all ages, religions and county origins and mainly men, though Switzers employed rather more women assistants. Here, too, the staff were all unmarried, except for two - Susie MacManus, the thirty year old book-keeper and a Director, Fred Switzer. Fred was a grandson of John Wright, and he also lived at no. 92 with his wife, Florence. It was the custom at Switzers for a member of the Board to live on the premises, to preserve the good order and discipline expected of those who worked in the drapery business.

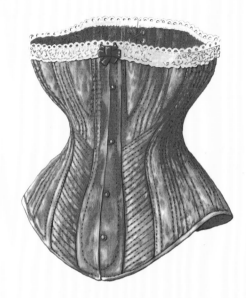

Above: *Corsets for the hourglass figure.*
Opposite: *The secret army; seamstresses at Brown Thomas.*

The age of Victoria, the great leap forward in technology and trade, was drawing to a close. The prosperous and mellow reigns of Edward VII and George V which followed reaped the harvest of all that often grim inventiveness and activity. That it was cut short so brutally by the First World War makes it all the more golden in nostalgic memory.

The phenomenon of the department store was now firmly established. Chicago had Marshall Fields, prominent in London were Whiteleys, Harrods, Marshall & Snelgroves and John Lewis. Paris had the Bon Marche.

Dublin had several - Clerys on Sackville Street, Arnotts on Henry Street, Pims on Sth. Great George's Street. And the jewels among them were Brown Thomas and Switzers, both on the city's finest shopping thoroughfare, Grafton Street.

There were other elegant and long-established shops, furriers, silk mercers, hatters and milliners on the street. But Brown Thomas and Switzers were true department stores, where everything could be bought under one roof. Villages almost in themselves, they were microcosms of the pleasant, busy, bustling town outside their doors.

Front of house in these bright emporia, commissionnaires in morning-coats ushered in the world to inspect the wares of the Empire. Assistants flitted from bale to bale of gleaming silks and sombre velvets and the air whispered with the rustle of skirts and the chink of coin. One among them was a charming young girl, Molly Allgood, soon to embark on a brilliant career as an actress at the newly-founded Abbey Theatre and to become the great love of John Millington Synge's tragically short life.

Off-stage, in the counting-house, clerks wrote copperplate in great ledgers, tailors and seamstresses sewed in the workrooms, cooks cooked, housemaids polished, porters carried, and horses, home from a laborious delivery up Howth Hill, were fed and watered in the stables in Clarendon Street.

Top: *The young Queen Victoria.*
Bottom: *Typical dress of the Victorian period.*
Opposite: *Preparing a substantial lunch for the department store "lodgers".*

The convulsions of the new century were not far off, war, rebellion, trade unionism and the fight for women's suffrage. For the moment however, men of business could bask in a prevailing atmosphere of stability and more or less unquestioned loyalty to the principle of steady profits.

Victoria, symbol of that stability, died in 1901. In April of the year before, the aged queen paid a last visit to her Irish kingdom. In Dublin, Royal visits were contentious events among the nationalist section of the population but the city always put up a great show of welcome on the day. Crowds turned out to cheer, bands played, and the Union Jack flew at every loyal window.

The merchants of Grafton Street were of course loyal to an exemplary degree and at Switzers the Board busily engaged itself with preparations for making the visit an appropriately splendid occasion.

Extensions had been contemplated and now they were embarked on. Mr Connolly, the builder, was consulted "with the object of ascertaining if a moderate premium would induce him to put on extra speed" so they could be ready on time. Sadly, Mr Connolly proved unable to finish before the Royal visit. However, the surge of celebratory shoppers could not be cheated of the new jewellery department, so an arch was opened in the partition. The new French shop-fittings could not be installed either so rough deal tables were substituted for counters and covered in crimson cloth.

It was an occasion when increased trade and healthy profits were not the primary consideration. Mr James Clements, the Managing Director, arranged that on the great day, Friday, staff should be given a "substantial" breakfast of bacon and eggs and a Dinner Tea in the afternoon. On the Saturday, the shop closed at 2 p.m. to allow the staff to attend the Queen's review of the splendid regiments of troops in the Phoenix Park, some of which would shortly be changing their red coats for a duller and more mundane khaki in South Africa.

Left: *Three ladies in costumes of the period.*
Opposite: *"I've warned you before…".*

Mr Clements was a member of the Masonic Order, as
John Wright Switzer had been and, apart from the effective
management of Switzers, his main interest was the orphan
schools of the Order. Typical of the Dublin businessman of
his time, he was sober, upright and paternalistic, a
dependable conduit between the humming human hive of
the shop and the Board of Directors. Everything was
referred to the Board, estimates for this and that, permission
for the special staff breakfast of eggs and bacon, ensuring
that not even the smallest expense was incurred without its
approval.

Generous towards the staff on momentous occasions like
the Queen's visit, Mr Clements was otherwise prudent. The
Board was informed that the lady assistants were using too
much bath water… A request from the apprentices for a
recreation room was deferred, at his suggestion, "until a
later date".

On the other hand, he asked the Board to permit hot water to be conveyed to the men's wash basins from the Engine Tank… At Whitsun he agreed to close the shop at 2 p.m. on the Saturday so that the assistants could spend the holiday in the country.… The Housekeeper, complaining of indifferent health, blamed the limited space of her sleeping and sitting rooms - the Milliners' workrooms were swopped with hers (workers like milliners and porters were ranked below assistants and housekeepers in shop hierarchies) and the Directors' dining-room was placed at her disposal to sit in the evenings.

Top: *Cocoa was the favourite drink of the late Victorian Age.*
Right: *A turn-of-the-century lady's walking gown.*
Opposite top: *Typical early twentieth century footwear.*
Opposite Bottom: *The dawn of a new century brought with it a craze for "the automobile". Switzers weren't slow to sell accessories to match.*

Though caution was an admired business virtue, the management of Switzers was adventurously forging ahead when it came to customer service and progressive improvements. In 1900 the first Public Telegraph Call Office was installed in the shop. Within a couple of years the motoring age was under way and its intrepid pioneers were being offered a selection of motor-car accessories and garments designed especially for motoring.

Victoria had detested the new machine. Her son, Edward VII, kept a fleet of Daimlers and brought them across the sea to tour the West of Ireland in 1903. John Samuel Switzer, grandson of John Wright Switzer and a Director, was a motoring enthusiast who is said to have been the first to own a motor-car in Ireland and brought his eight year old son Ernest to watch the Gordon Bennett Race in the same year.

The occasional De Dion Bouton or Panhard could now be seen charging, as it must have seemed to the awed spectator, up and down Grafton Street. Switzers advertised their motor specialities. Leather aprons, goggles, gauntlets, peaked caps, motorcoats; and for ladies, hoods and yashmaks in waterproof silk, as cumbersome and almost as hermetically sealed as the headgear later worn by spacemen. Early in the century, Switzers invested in a motorised delivery van, an Argyll, and in 1910 bought a second.

But Grafton Street was still mainly a sociable street of strollers and horse-drawn carriages. In the high meridian of Edwardian stability, it was the street where the city's leisured classes, under the awnings hung out to shade pedestrians from the effulgent Edwardian sun, mingled with officials from the Administration, country landowners in town for a few days at the Club, and officers on leave from India and distant outposts of the Empire.

Hats were doffed in greeting to handsome ladies turning into Brown Thomas to be fitted for a new gown, pleasant mornings were passed browsing in the best shops, and then to one of the elegant tea and coffee rooms for a plate of muffins or ices, depending on the season.

  Among the hatters, shirt and collar makers, booksellers,
and boot and shoe makers lining the street were shops with
goods to suit the most whimsical taste. Knaggs Bros. had the
Irish Bog Oak Works at no. 27 with an interesting line in
jewellery made of bog oak, inset with jet, silver and gold.
Madame Mangotti, Naturalist, at no. 32, specialised in the
"feathered tribes". She kept singing birds from near and far,
including the sweetest warblers from the Harz mountains in
Prussia. At no. 10 was "the daily resort of all that is
aristocratic and wealthy", Mitchell's Confectioners. There,
the smart-set of Dublin society, dressed in confections to
rival Mitchell's own, and surrounded by their smaller
parcels that could be taken home on the tram, consumed
trembling jellies served on cut-glass dishes while the slow
pop of champagne corks punctuated the chatter of gossip
and repartee.

Leopold Bloom, probably the best-known stroller in fiction, decided on a more hearty lunch of gorgonzola and red wine in Davy Byrnes of Duke Street on that golden day of the 16th of June 1904, immortalised by James Joyce. On his way there, he turned into Grafton Street, paused at Yeates the Opticians on the corner, pricing the field-glasses and, musing, went on.

Lost in erotic reverie, he passed Adam Court. Here, the street, "gay with housed awnings, lured his senses"…

"Muslin prints, silkdames and dowagers, jingle of harnesses, hoofthuds lowringing in the baking causeway…"

He passed, "dallying, the windows of Brown Thomas, silk mercers", where "a tilted urn poured from its mouth a flood of bloodhued poplin. Lustrous blood".

The window display, even then recherche, incited in him sensuous longings. "Gleaming silks, petticoats on slim brass rails, rays of flat silk stockings"…

"Cascades of ribbons. Flimsy China silks…. Pincushions". The pincushions restore him to more mundane thoughts and he remembers Mollie at home in Eccles Street and how, for lack of a pincushion, she sticks stray pins in the curtains. Perhaps for her birthday, three months off, he will buy her a pincushion…

"High voices. Sunwarm silk. Jingling harnesses. All for a woman, home and houses, silkwebs, silver, rich fruits spicy from Jaffa…Agendath Netaim. Wealth of the world".

Bloom's gaze into the window of Brown Thomas confirms the difference in character which was already apparent between Brown Thomas and Switzers. Switzers was a first-class department store offering quality goods of all descriptions and with a rather practical image. Brown Thomas on the other hand was a connoisseur's delight, where one could wander among items of luxury and elegance, apparel appealing to the imagination and the senses.

Behind the scenes of this world however, in which everyone was expected to endeavour to be happy in his or her estate, the rumbles of mutiny were beginning to be heard. In the harsher Victorian age, a position in drapery was regarded as a very superior occupation and a boy or girl of the respectable classes who was granted an apprenticeship (for a fee) at a prestigious house like Brown Thomas or Switzers was considered exceedingly lucky. The long hours and low wages should be accepted with gratitude.

In comparison with the teeming hungry poor, they were certainly fortunate. But in the new progressive century, they expected more.

The Drapers' Assistants' Association was formed in 1904 and began a campaign to improve the lives of shop assistants. Their journal, *The Drapers' Assistant*, written in the rhetorical and colourfully militant language of the time, painted a sad picture of the life of the overworked, underpaid draper's assistant and the "pernicious customs" he, and increasingly she, were expected to accept without protest.

It was a life of "abject slavery", it claimed. It spoke optimistically of what "a few years combination and education" would inevitably achieve, a hint which the opposition, the Merchant Drapers' Association, was not yet inclined to take at all seriously. The assistants' grievances were many.

They worked six days in the week and wanted a weekly half-holiday. They wanted regulated opening hours and payment for overtime. They wanted an end to the employer's option of instant dismissal and to the apprenticeship system. Pensions, annual holidays and sick pay were of course still distant dreams.

The living-in system was the target of the most impassioned and bitter rhetoric. Not only did the unfortunate assistant who lived in have to eat "clerk's butter" (margarine) and "poor-law loaf" but he also had to buy his own candles, soap and polish. And worse - this was cleverly couched in a high moral tone - he had to "share with undesirables", such as "the drunkard, the profaner, the immoral, the spy". Later on, the "undesirable" would become the tubercular assistant, for whom *The Drapers' Assistant* showed surprisingly little pity.

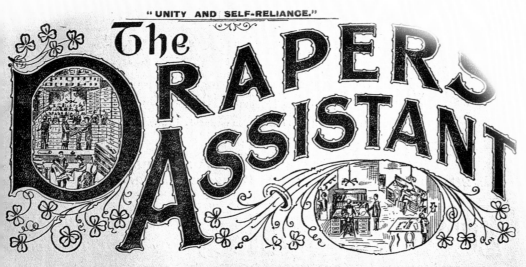

"UNITY AND SELF-RELIANCE."

The DRAPERS ASSISTANT

THE OFFICIAL JOURNAL OF THE IRISH DRAPERS' ASSISTANTS' BENEFIT AND PROTECTIVE ASSOCIATION.

Top: *A black frock trimmed with Irish lace.*
Left: *The Drapers' Assistants' "mouthpiece".*
Opposite: *"Social life" at Switzers.*

"Talking of some of the Dublin drapery stores" wrote the journal, "we really think the bigger the establishment, the more barrack-like the life. We know of one house in St. Stephen's Green where fifty young men and women board and not a single bath for them - and the public baths close at 8 p.m." Was it talking of Switzers, who had a house in St. Stephen's Green where some of its assistants lived?

The assistant lived on cold meat and rice cooked in water and treacle, it said. And not only was he hungry, but the poor assistant had a lonely life as well, counting every penny, unable to marry because he couldn't afford to, working late and then going straight back to a comfortless bedroom, uncurtained and with a cold grate.

It was possibly not that lonely. Keen observers have suggested that the notable depression in the floorboards of the corridor between the men's and women's dormitories in Switzers was a result of the sociable traffic from one to the other.

The Drapers' Assistant described the strictures of dormitory life for grown men and women. The fine system could have been formulated by a schoolmaster like Mr Gradgrind - 6d for unnecessary talking in the bedrooms, 3d for leaving an article of clothing in the room, 1s. for not turning off the gas, 2/6 for sleeping out without a signed docket, 5s. for using matches and lighting paper, 2d for losing your copy of the rules…

Early closing at 2 p.m. on Saturdays to give assistants a half-holiday was in 1904 considered an idle dream. But the assistants took to regularly parading draped in white sheets with a clock depicted front and rear showing the magic hour of 2.

In 1912 the weekly half-holiday was universally adopted. In 1910, the Shops Bill was passed, limiting working hours to 60 per week. And in the same year, Switzers' staff - Buyers, Superintendents, Assistants, Clerks and Porters - were given one or two weeks annual holidays, depending on length of service.

By 1913, Brown Thomas had no longer any live-in assistants. In Switzers, some continued to live in the attic rooms right up to the 1940s.

Switzers' management, especially, was sorely tried by the Drapers' Assistants' Association. In March 1910, Mr Clements reported to the Board that Mr O'Reilly of the Silk Department proposed marrying and was seeking a week's holidays. When the Board discovered that the young lady he intended to marry owned a business similar to Switzers', Mr O'Reilly was dismissed.

It was a strange decision. Mr O'Reilly had been with Switzers for sixteen years and his bride's small establishment on the Lower Drumcondra Road was unlikely to be in a position to compete with the great store on Grafton Street, all of which was pointed out at length in *The Drapers' Assistant*.

The controversy about Mr O'Reilly, publicised by the indignant Association, was hot, heavy and long-lived.

"Thou Shalt Not Marry", cried the headlines. Switzer's Board of Directors, "sitting in the august gloom of their chambers in Grafton Street" were cast as advocates of involuntary celibacy. In August, there was a public meeting at the Rotunda attended by several Members of Parliament and the redoubtable feminist, Hannah Sheehy-Skeffington. Switzers received a deputation of concerned customers and was obliged to send a telegram stating its case to the *London Opinion* magazine.

Opposite page: *The issue of early closing was always a contentious one.*

But the shop remained firm. Mr O'Reilly went off to Drumcondra and the issue faded away, though not in the eyes of the Drapers' Assistants' Association. Switzers continued to be portrayed as something of a bête noir in the columns of its journal for years afterwards.

Mr Clements and his Board rode out the storm, keeping pace with modern developments more pertinent, as they saw it, to the shop's progress. The glorious new shop front on Wicklow Street, a beautiful example of art nouveau, was unveiled. A magnificent French stairs, free-hanging and wending an opulent curved path up to the galleries on the third floor, was installed.

In 1911 Mr Clements took one of the new vacuum cleaners on trial and a new public telephone call box was erected. It was decided that staff should wear a uniform colour, black being considered the most appropriate. Then Mr Clements fell ill and retired to Valentia to recuperate.

Brown Thomas was not so prone to controversy. Indeed when Brown Thomas was mentioned in *The Drapers' Assistant*, it was in approving tones.

In October 1907, rather late in comparison with other successful shops, it was formed into a public company. Vere Ward Brown, son of the founder, was elected Chairman but he fell ill and died in the August of the same year. Hugh Brown, Vere's brother and a Pastor in the Baptist Ministry, therefore became the first Chairman of Brown Thomas & Co. Ltd. Mr Joseph Fitzgerald, the General Manager of long-standing, was also on the Board. The Company's auditors were Craig Gardner.

Opposite: *The Switzer Wicklow Street entrance circa 1911.*

Sports costumes for ladies was the newest vogue. The voluminous style, bustled, ruffled and furbelowed had given way to a graceful silhouette, cut lean and simple. Brown Thomas had the newest patterns from London (which had replaced Paris as the centre of the fashion world) in tennis dresses, archery, rinking and golfing outfits. For Autumn in 1912, sportswear was recommended to be of white velvet corduroy, cut quite short, enabling a pair of neat high-laced boots to be seen. The new coat had capacious outside pockets - "quite indispensable for the sportswoman's gear".

In June every year, the "Graftons" had a sports-day when there were inter-house competitions. In 1912, Mr James Lawlor was badly missed by the Switzer side as he had left to take up a position at Todd Burns and was no longer a Grafton.

There was a new vogue too in corsetry. Some women were now wearing separate bust and hip corsets, instead of an all-embracing one. The possibility that within fifty years, many women would be wearing none at all would have seemed outrageous. An elaborate hat was however still essential.

Top and left: *Two of the most popular games in the Brown Thomas inter-house sports tournament.*
Opposite: *The scroll presented to Joseph Fitzgerald, illuminated by J. Hopkins.*
Address to J.G. Fitzgerald, Esq. "We the employees of above firm feel that we cannot allow the present occasion to pass without expressing in some degree our deep sense of the kindness and consideration which we have always received at your hands in granting us the great boon of a summer holiday as a free gift..."
July 1887

A note of religious devoutness and a rather less businesslike approach than at Switzers is perceptible in these weekly meetings of the new Brown Thomas Board. Often the sole agenda was the consideration of charitable requests and these were nearly always approved.

City of Dublin Hospitals' subscriptions were annually passed and signed. Prudent sums were disbursed to organisations ranging from the Sisters of Mercy at Baggot Street to the Sick and Indigent Roomkeepers, Aged Governesses and Distressed Protestants.

There was often of course a practical quid pro quo implicit in these donations. Regarding an application for a subscription from St. John's House of Rest, a letter was composed to Miss French of St. John's to say that a cheque had duly been passed and signed. It was however pointed out to Miss French that the cheque had been held over "owing to the discourteous manner in which their representative was received when he called in the usual way of business".

The Directors at Brown Thomas were not at all as involved as at Switzers in the day to day running of the shop. There is an impression that their minds were on loftier things. When the Managing Director of 30 years, Mr Joseph Fitzgerald, tendered his resignation in 1913, the Board voted him heartfelt thanks for his splendid and faithful services for so many years. "We earnestly pray God may speedily restore Mr Fitzgerald to his normal state of health".

The mind of the Brown Thomas Chairman, Pastor Hugh Brown, was indeed on loftier things. His father, Hugh, had been a trustee of the Zion Church in Rathgar, though not fanatically religious. Neither were Pastor Hugh's brothers Vere Ward and Robert. Vere had been the most committed to Brown Thomas while Robert had studied medicine at Trinity and founded a clinic, Maison de la Santé, on Charlemont Street. He was also an urban councillor, a Justice of the Peace and a keen yachtsman who sailed from Kingstown to St. Petersburg. Pastor Hugh was a Barrister who gave up the law to become a Baptist minister. He was deeply evangelical.

His mother, Marianne, had inherited a fortune from her husband. Some years after his death, she built a fine house, "Stratford" and Hugh, who was unmarried, lived with her. He, in the words of his great-nephew, Alan Brown, "got carried away with the Baptists" and persuaded the indulgent Marianne to part with enormous sums on behalf of the Church.

She financed a Baptist Chapel in Harcourt Street and another in Phibsboro, laying the foundation stones of both with an ivory-handled engraved silver trowel. Marianne financed the journeys of Church Elders to New Zealand, Australia and the "deep South" of the United States to visit distant Church members.

Her fortune was, as family lore puts it, "going down the Baptist pipes". In 1910, she was in debt to the company and was charged 5% interest per £1000. In the same year, Pastor Hugh requested that he and Mr Fitzgerald be jointly appointed Managing Director at annual salaries of £300 and £700 respectively. In 1911 he asked that the family discount of 2½% wholesale be increased and was negotiating to sell some of his shares in Brown Thomas.

In January 1912, Marianne Brown died in her sleep at the age of 85. The Board recorded that she "abounded in good deeds and generous impulses". Her indebtedness to Brown Thomas brought about a change in its management and overall control.

In May, Robert Brown announced that "due to social and family reasons precipitated by the death of his dear mother, he and the family of the late Mrs Vere Ward Brown had resolved to sell their ordinary shares in the Company". The buyer was Mr John Purcell of North Earl Street, a former tobacconist. Pastor Hugh Brown, who had moved to the Shelbourne Hotel, had also arranged to sell his ordinary shares to Mr Purcell.

With all the Ordinary shares in the Company in his possession, Mr Purcell became Chairman. Mr Fitzgerald was retained as Managing Director though at a reduced salary of £600. The Brown family retained their Preference Shares and Hugh was allowed a salary of £100 to represent their interests on the Board. But they had effectively ceded control of Brown Thomas to John Purcell. Pastor Hugh met the Buyers and Superintendents to inform them of the new developments, "thanked them for their courtesy and loyalty and recommended Mr Purcell as worthy of similar treatment at their hands".

Under Mr Purcell, Board meetings had a more businesslike and thoroughgoing flavour. There were attempts to cut costs. When Mr Fitzgerald died, the manager, Mr Woollard, who was promoted to replace him as Managing Director, was allowed an annual salary of £425.

In 1914, annual pew rents to the Molyneux Church were discontinued. There were no longer any resident assistants to occupy them - something which met with the approval of the Drapers' Assistants' Association - but also because Mr Purcell did not share Pastor Hugh Brown's preoccupations.

Above: *Zion Church, Rathgar.*
Opposite: *The Brown Family, 1894, Back row, left to right - Nancy Weir, Marianne Brown, Robert Brown, Frances Brown.*
Front row, left to right - Percy Brown, Frank Brown, taken at "Hopeton", Terenure Road East.

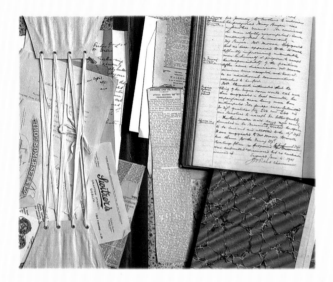

An item commonly on the agenda of both shops was Overdue Accounts. Marchioness Coyngham's was discussed at Brown Thomas; Lady Campbell wrote to Switzers protesting at being pressed for hers. New gowns were always in demand for the levees at the Castle but ladies were often disinclined to pay for them. Managements were torn between the wish to keep their important customers and the wish to be paid. In 1914, Brown Thomas took the extremely unusual step of instituting legal proceedings against a Mr Wainwright Crowe of Ennis to recover the debts on his account. Generally, patience and good grace was the attitude towards outstanding accounts.

At a time when benefits such as pensions and sick pay to staff were at the discretion of the Board, these were often topics, and letters from grateful recipients or relations noted with satisfaction. At Brown Thomas, the Warehouse and Counting House staffs contributed £13/7/0 to the family of the late Michael Lambert, delivery porter. The Board resolved to contribute "a like sum from the firm".

Reading between the lines of some cursorily noted decisions of reductions or discontinuance of payments, small everyday tragedies can be imagined. "Resolved that the pension of £24 per annum now paid to Mr Thomas A. White be discontinued… That the weekly payment to Miss Butler, absent for 16 weeks owing to ill-health be reduced to 10/-…" Would the names of Mr White and Miss Butler be seen before long on the lists of the Distressed Protestants or the Old Men's Asylum?

Above: *Switzers kept meticulous records of all transactions.*
Opposite: *Many Switzers and Brown Thomas staff took part in the war to end all wars.*

By August 1914, Britain - and Ireland - were at war with
Germany. The First World War, which was to cause such
upheavals in European life, had begun its long and agonising
course.

Almost immediately its reality was felt in a sudden
downturn in business. Customers had taken fright and were
purchasing with caution. Brown Thomas postponed the new
Hot Water Installations, intended to be put in for the winter.
Assistants' commissions on orders over £100 were reduced
to 1¼%.

At Switzers it was decided to reduce all salaries by 20%
because of poor trading. Shareholders, it was added, would
not receive dividends. The cut in salaries elicited a letter of
protest from the Drapers' Assistants' Association but because
it had been amicably arranged after a meeting with the staff,
this was given scant attention.

By the Autumn, an army recruitment drive was gathering
force.

Above: *The recruiting officer - Switzers and Brown Thomas were eager to support the war effort.*

In October, both shops received letters from the Recruiting Committee, requesting an encouraging attitude from employers. Switzers agreed that the situation of anyone joining the army would be kept open until his return from active service. In the case of married men there would be weekly allowances for their wives and children. Later, anyone, married or single who joined up was given half-pay for the duration of his army service.

At Brown Thomas, situations were also held open, although the matter of salary was to be considered in each individual case. Trained nurses were to be charged for their purchases at wholesale prices.

These inducements must have been very tempting to a young man living a constricted life as a draper's assistant or clerk and inflamed with war-fever and the scent of adventure. Soon, lady assistants were being drafted into the departments normally run by men. New apprentices were taken on at Brown Thomas at a brisk rate. Switzers was sufficiently alarmed at the extent of the departures to the Front to insist that assistants contemplating joining the army must first get permission from the Board.

The war, however presented an undeniable business opportunity. Switzers quickly became foremost among suppliers of military wear for officers. In November 1914, its new department for Soldiers' Comforts was opened.

Within a year, they were supplying "complete military outfits for the winter campaign - folding bedsteads, kit-bags" and "the best mitt for the trenches". Brown Thomas too had "warm comforts for soldiers and sailors; army blankets, woollen garments and mittens".

Trading returned to its former briskness. Early in 1915, the assistants' salaries at Switzers were restored to the former rate and at the annual meeting, staff were thanked for their loyal services. There was not, shareholders were assured, "a more contented and courteous body of officials to be found in any establishment in Dublin". They were also assured that the Directors had "made every arrangement for and offered every encouragement to the members of the staff to join the King's Colours".

The Brown Thomas Board suggested to Mr McNichol who canvassed hotels and hospitals for their linen and calico supplies, that he should include in his canvas their Army blankets.

Percy Brown, son of Robert, reading law at Trinity, was in the College Officers' Training Corps. When the Corps was addressed by Willy Redmond and promised Home Rule, he joined up. He would be awarded an M.C. but would also return badly shaken by his experiences.

It was Brown Thomas which had the first acquaintance with the tragedies of war. In November 1914, Captain Frederick Brown of the 101st Grenadiers, son of Vere Ward Brown and first cousin of Percy, was killed in East Africa. And the brother of a Mr Keogh, assistant, was killed in action in France in the same month.

Above: *The Recruiting Post at Grattan's statue.*
Left: *A war-time scene in College Green.*

Fashion, declared the columnists, would not change until peace was proclaimed. But this noble renunciation did not last very long. Town girls who were encouraged to work on farms for their holidays could wear, it was suggested, wide leather belts to hold in their coats and breeches. This contrivance could look "very becoming". It was an early example of "military style".

Throughout the war, Brown Thomas and Switzers advertised "the new rest-gowns" and "debs gowns" for young ladies and Eton outfits for boys. Brown Thomas opened its new warerooms in Duke Street and Switzers began the manufacture of shirts in their workrooms. It was during the war that proposals for the Tea-Rooms and the Times Library at Switzers were considered and approved.

However, in spite of their best efforts, it could not be business as usual. Donations now were largely to hospitals for wounded soldiers such as Jervis Street and Monkstown. Switzers gave Lady Robinson "a piece of furniture to the value of £2" for a sale in aid of prisoners in Germany; Lady Mayo was given linen to the value of 10/- for a stall for the Dublin Fusiliers. In Christmas week 1915, when there was an influx of wounded from the Irish regiments in the Dardanelles, the premises at 87 Grafton Street were placed at the disposal of the Red Cross for the use of soldiers.

Top: *A recruitment poster, circa 1915.*
Left: *Wounded soldiers from the Irish Regiments return home.*
Opposite: *Inside the GPO, Easter Week 1916.*

In the early months of the war, a customer complained to
Switzers that they had in their employment an assistant, Mr
Nanz, who was of enemy nationality. Mr Nanz had to resign
in the following May when Switzers signed an agreement
with the anti-German Union not to employ German labour.
It was wondered whether it would be necessary to insure
against aircraft bombardment.

Mrs Goff's plans for soldiers' teas at no. 87 Grafton Street
during Easter week were abruptly disrupted.

On the morning of Monday, April 24th 1916, when Mrs
Goff would have been laying the tables, the Rising began,
bringing normal business to a halt for the week it lasted.

At its end, when the rebels surrendered, Sackville Street,
where the heaviest fighting took place, was a wasteland. But
Grafton Street emerged unscathed. All around, there had
been fires and bombardments. But as the buildings on
Grafton Street escaped occupation, they escaped
destruction.

During the "recent disturbances", Mr Clements reported
to the Board of Switzers when it was all over, the premises
had not suffered any damage. In magnanimous mood, the
Board agreed to pay salaries in full to the assistants and
heads of workrooms for the days they had been unable to be
at their posts.

Aware that they had been lucky and that the disturbances
might recur in the future, Mr Clements was asked to make
enquiries about the cost of insurance against riot and
rebellion. Sprinklers used by Arnotts and other shops that
had been set alight had not proved a great success and it was
decided not to install them in Switzers.

But the war in Europe still went on. Staff shortages continued to be a problem. When, in 1918, it seemed that conscription would be extended to Ireland, Mr Avison, the new managing director (the hard-working and devoted Mr Clements had died) was asked to seek information about the Switzers position on staff liable to be called up. The Board seemed less than enthusiastic about Switzers being asked to provide the Army with yet more of its staff. Mr Avison reported that "no legal obligation lay with them to inform the authorities".

Times were getting better for his staff. Assistants got a minimum wage agreement in June 1918; and in October an earlier closing time of 5.30, allowing them to be away by 6.

The war was responsible for a steady rise in inflation but it also brought good business. Indeed, turnover was so much higher in 1917 and 1918 that Switzers had amassed a healthy reserve of £52,000 - partly perhaps because profits had been under-estimated to avoid heavy war-time Government taxes. It was decided to capitalise on this by giving each shareholder two extra five-pound shares for each one they already held. And, always up-to-the-minute with modern technology, a complete vacuum-cleaning plant was installed.

At last, in November 1918 - at the eleventh hour of the eleventh day of the eleventh month, the Armistice came into effect. World War I was over. 49,000 Irishmen had died in action. Among them were several employees of Switzers and Brown Thomas.

In Ireland however another war was about to break out. Since the Rising, the separatist movement had been gaining strength. With the killing of two policemen at Soloheadbeg in Co. Tipperary in 1919, active hostilities began. Years of turbulence were to ensue. But as had been the case with the Great War, the motto of the commercial world was to be, in so far as was possible, business as usual.

Top: *"The countless white crosses in mute witness stand..."*
Above: *The Black & Tans strike fear into the hearts of Dubliners during the War of Independence.*

Switzers opened the Times Library, with its fine mahogany fittings, in 1918. This was a lending-library, the books provided by the Times Library Service in London. For an annual subscription of one guinea upwards, members could browse among shelves of the most modern editions, have books delivered by a Switzers van or dispatched to them by post. The postal service was especially popular among country members.

The jazzy mood of the Twenties arrived at Switzers in 1919 in the shape of two palms, purchased from Jamesons. Palms were one of the essential decorating accessories of the decade, when cocktails were sipped in Palm Courts everywhere and music ensembles played the latest numbers under the spreading leaves of hothouse palms.

It was also the mood however of regular outbreaks of "trouble in the House". Inflation, and strengthening trade unionism, were causing alarming demands for increases in salaries. A tailors' strike was settled with an ex gratia payment. But by February the Board voted themselves an extra £250 per annum, and war bonuses all round, to be followed by general increases in salary. Piece-workers like tailors, tailoresses, cabinet-makers and charwomen were excluded at first from the war-bonus scale but after Union pressure were brought in.

In 1921, staff objected to the employment of non-union employees and threatened to strike if offending assistants were not compelled to join the Union. They did strike, culminating in a two day lock-out. A conference was held in the Mansion House at which the Lord Mayor presided. When the Board requested all workers to join the union, work resumed.

And live-in assistants could no longer claim to be subsisting on a Dickensian diet of treacled rice and cold potatoes. In the early 1920s their complaint was that they were being fed too much salmon!

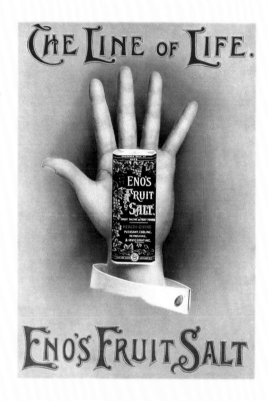

Top: *Advertising took on the brashness of the twenties, setting trends which remain with us to this day.*
Above: *The Jazz Age comes to Switzers.*

At Brown Thomas in 1919, far-reaching changes occurred. John Purcell died in 1919 and the shop changed hands. The man who bought it was the legendary American, Harry Gordon Selfridge. Selfridge cannot be credited with inventing the department store, but he was certainly its most visionary exponent.

Selfridge began his retail career as a stock boy in the 1880s in one of the first great stores, Marshall Fields of Chicago. Within a few years, he was persuading an often reluctant Marshall Field, its owner, to experiment with some of the innovative ideas which seemed to tumble daily from his fertile brain. Inevitably successful, they were, over the years, to transform department stores everywhere.

The annual sale, the bargain basement, displays of goods accessible to the customer so she could handle them freely before speaking to an assistant, eye-catching advertising splashes in the newspapers - all these were Selfridge innovations. Debonair, full of dash and go, seeming to fly about Marshall Fields, he was known as "Mile A Minute" Harry.

Early in the 1900s, Selfridge left Chicago and came to London, where, in 1909, he opened Selfridge & Co. in Oxford Street. At his store, there were no more floor-walkers, in their tails and striped trousers to inhibit the atmosphere of relaxed browsing - and impulse buying. It was presented as a club, a social and leisure centre, with the opportunity to purchase things being an additional facility. There were writing, reading and rest-rooms, a post office, a roof-garden, all at your disposal whether you bought something or not.

Top: *As the political situation stabilised, Dublin found a new Gaelic confidence as depicted in the above Cantwell's coffee and chicory advertisement. Note the elaborate celtic designs.*
Left: *Third from left, Harry "Mile-a-Minute" Selfridge on the first commercial flight from London to Baldonnel, June 1919.*

When the colourful and extravagant Gordon Selfridge bought Brown Thomas in 1919 as one of his many provincial acquisitions, he took over from men with a very different character to his. Devout, genteel and prudent as they were however, they had continued the shop's long tradition of elegance and exclusivity. At this point, in the leaner, freer, more democratic post-war era, Selfridge was just the man it needed to revitalise its image and its finances.

Brown Thomas's Victorian letterhead, incorporating the Royal motto, "Honi Soit Qui Mal Y Pense" was replaced by the modernist looking Selfridge key. Advertising had never been a priority for Brown Thomas. Now discreet advertisements were placed strategically in places frequented by its customers - hotels like the Hibernian, the Shelbourne and the Gresham; or in appropriate publications - the Kingstown and Monkstown parish magazines and the *Irish Clergy List*.

Under Selfridge, they now, like Switzers had done before them, took half-page spreads in the daily newspapers, advertising their seasonal sales, their Christmas specials, the latest models in winter coats and frocks... the terms "mantle" and "gown" of the pre-war were becoming obsolete. Brown Thomas was diversifying its appeal.

Just as in London's Selfridges, a writing-room was set up in Brown Thomas, with headed writing-paper supplied, which Dubliners were urged to regard as their club. And it was no longer merely a silk-mercers or a superior drapers. A household department appeared, selling china and household implements. Within a few years, Brown Thomas was selling modern "hardware" like bicycles and wireless sets.

Top and Right: *In line with trends at the time, in the early 1920s, Brown Thomas diversified into sports and leisure goods.*

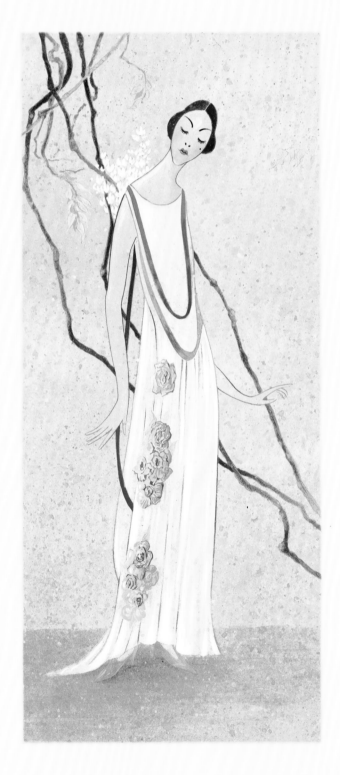

In the prevailing climate in Ireland of turmoil and political instability this was not a particularly auspicious time for a purchase like Brown Thomas. But only in the most extreme circumstances did shoppers stop shopping and shops reluctantly close their doors to them.

Switzers opened a new American-style Soda Fountain in 1921, serving delights like Yama Yama, Pink Lady and Hug Me Tight. The Jazz Age was on its way. But it was generally agreed among all the Drapery Houses at the end of 1921 that the past year had been one of the most trying and difficult for the trade. In May, a new Viceroy, Viscount FitzAlan, had been sworn in. He would be the last.

"Greater changes than ever before have taken place in Ireland during the year", Switzers' chairman, Mr Gibson Moore, told the Annual General Meeting. "We hope that some good may develop out of it for the good of the country that might result in more security for life and property…"

Dublin had been isolated and the unsettled state of the country which curtailed travelling, had hindered "the maintaining of the very successful results of the previous year's trading".

High wages were an even greater cause for concern. "They must come down", said Mr Moore. They had forced up prices, "so much that people would not buy and this way the workers are being hit themselves".

At the Henry Street Warehouse, there was consternation among the Directors that the wages bill amounted to £5000 more than in the previous year. In a few months, it was suggested, there would have to be a general lock-out on the part of the trade.

Left: *A typical '20s "Flapper".*
Opposite Top: *Michael Collins, Commander of the pro-Treaty forces.*
Opposite Bottom: *The destruction of the Four Courts, Dublin, Friday, 30th June 1922 marked the real start of the Civil War.*

In January 1922, with the signing of the Anglo-Irish Treaty, the war of independence came to an end and Michael Collins took formal control of Dublin Castle from Viscount FitzAlan. The old order was rapidly fading away. But before the new regime could fully assert itself, a further conflict had to be fought.

In March, the anti-treaty side occupied the Four Courts. Early in the morning of the 28th of June, the bombardment of the building by the Free State Government Forces began. Intense street fighting continued for days, centred again around O'Connell Street, formerly Sackville Street. It was a situation that the shops could not ignore, even on Grafton Street.

At 5 p.m. on the 28th, Switzers closed the premises and did not re-open for normal trading until the 7th of July. All the other shops did the same, although they were in daily contact with each other about the advisability of opening from day to day. On the 5th, Switzers' stalwarts, the Managing Director, Mr Avison, Director Fred Switzer, even the 85 year old Chairman, Mr Gibson Moore, were present and opened the store briefly. They had to concede there was no business to be done.

On the 7th damages were assessed at £568/15/2 and then it was back to business as usual. It was decided that the Soda Fountain and The Tea Rooms should be amalgamated into one department.

Turbulence and hostilities continued through 1923. But by the end of the year, a recognition of the new status quo was established, the situation was calmer and Ireland was settling into its new identity as an independent state.

"For the first time in many years", declared Sir James Percy at the Annual Meeting, standing in for Mr Gibson Moore, "it is felt we can have confidence in the future of the country. We have men at the head of affairs who have courage and are going to give us good government and this will affect every business not only in Dublin but throughout Ireland…"

Despite this vocal support for the Government of the day, Switzers always maintained a non-partisan attitude. In 1926, when a representative from Cumann na nGaedhal, the Government Party, called asking for a subscription, the Board refused on the grounds that "we do not take sides in party politics".

After the tragedies and animosities of years of conflict, the 1920s were not a particularly happy or prosperous time in Ireland. But this was, after all, the Jazz Age and though Dublin could not be said to be at the centre of the fun, there was a certain sense of liberation and excitement. The old-world glamour of the Anglo-Irish aristocracy and the Viceregal court had vanished but a fresh new style of modernity was rapidly replacing it. New habits of social and cultural life were forming around the theatres, ballrooms, music-clubs and the new craze, the cinema. Now, the ruling class sat in the Dail and Senate in Leinster House and just as power had passed into the hands of new classes, so too did money.

There were enough people of wealth and leisure for
Grafton Street to continue to bloom as a place for shopping
and conversation. The Saturday morning stroll on Grafton
Street was by now an established feature of Dublin life. But
even on weekdays it was thronged, the place to see and be
seen.

Although still regarded as an exclusive thoroughfare,
shopping in Grafton Street had become a more democratic
activity. Woolworths had a large store at the upper end of
the street. Picture-goers piled into the Grafton Cinema
close by to see the new talkies. Lower down, beyond Brown
Thomas, Mitchells was still a rendezvous for lunching
Southside ladies. Bewley's Oriental Cafe and Robert's Cafe
were the haunts of students from Trinity and the
comparatively new National University who made up a
substantial part of the Grafton Street concourse.

At Jammets famous restaurant in Frenchman's Lane, the
theatrical set mingled with survivors of the aristocracy,
intellectuals, and the more bohemian officials and
professionals. Later on in the night, they might be seen in
Madame Toto Cogley's new nightclub at the top of the
street.

The modern age had arrived. Hemlines rose, garments
were lean, sleek and functional, hair was bobbed and
marcel-waved. The fashionable young woman wore long-
waisted short dresses almost skimming the knee, lots of
lipstick, adored Jazz, danced the Charleston, and had no
objection to being considered "fast". Youth culture was born.

Quick to service the new trend for cutting and waving
hair, Switzers opened a new Hairdressing Salon in 1926.
Shampoo stands were purchased for £11 each, a Turkish
carpet for £34/2/6 and a London hairdresser, suitably called
Mr Lovely, was engaged at £7 a week.

The Derby hat currently worn by men was being discarded in favour of no hat at all as it was a nuisance getting in and out of motor-cars. In 1926, there were so many motor-cars that they were blocking Wicklow Street and in Switzers' opinion, were impeding trade. The era of traffic-jams and parking-headaches had begun.

Switzers itself was adding to the congestion. In 1924, a Morris Cowley was bought for the Traveller and in 1926, was traded in for a Fiat. In 1925, their horses were finally put out to grass. In that year, after a horse-drawn delivery van was involved in an accident on the Stillorgan Road, all the remaining horse vans were replaced by motorised versions, painted by Rawson's Garages in blue and white and with a fresh italic Switzers logo. The stables in Clarendon Street were re-constructed into garages to house the new vans.

Buyers however still travelled by train and were now advised that they could no longer travel first class as they had since the war. They should travel third class or saloon now that the wartime mêlée had subsided.

In its new Chairman, John Samuel Switzer, the shop again had a Switzer as chairman. The Soda Fountain was expanded into a full Restaurant and Grill Room, serving luncheon and afternoon tea. It had a modern décor - oak ceiling, frieze rail in serpent blue, and neutral walls hung with handsome prints of Old Dublin. Customers enjoyed the use of linen table napkins, although not because they were more attractive. They had proved vastly more economic than paper napkins.

ABOVE: *Motor cars of the day which caused such headaches.*
Right: *From the Switzer archive; the arrival of the very distinctive Switzers delivery van.*

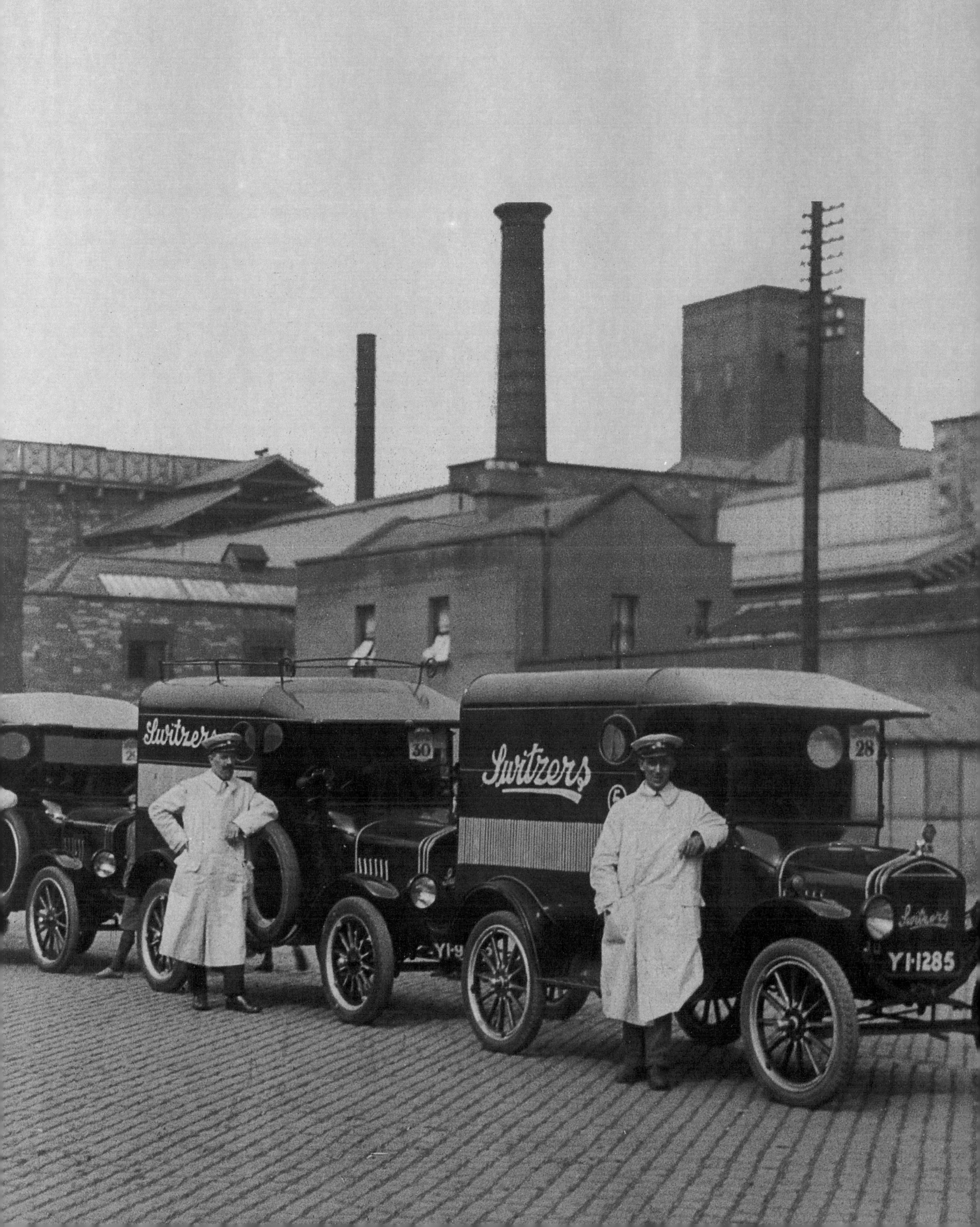
Switzers
30
Switzers
28
Switzers
YI·1285

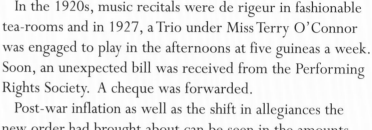

Ireland's Link with America

In the 1920s, music recitals were de rigeur in fashionable tea-rooms and in 1927, a Trio under Miss Terry O'Connor was engaged to play in the afternoons at five guineas a week. Soon, an unexpected bill was received from the Performing Rights Society. A cheque was forwarded.

Post-war inflation as well as the shift in allegiances the new order had brought about can be seen in the amounts and destinations of charitable donations during the Twenties. £25 was voted to the Wesley College War Memorial, £25 to the Tailteann Games in 1926, £10 to the staff for their Charabanc Picnic, ten guineas to *The Irish Times* special fuel fund during the fuel strike. And £25 to the Taoiseach, W.T. Cosgrave's Relief Fund for the disaster at Drumcollogher, Co. Limerick, when 49 people died in a fire at the cinema as they watched a showing of The Ten Commandments.

The pre-war distaste for indebtedness was being gradually undermined. You could now buy a Hoover vacuum cleaner at Switzers on the Hire Purchase system. But a suggestion that this facility be extended to the Ciro Pearls department was looked on with great disfavour. A vacuum cleaner was a sensible buy by a sensible woman. The sort of person who bought pearls on hire purchase might be less reliable.

The smoking of cigarettes in public had been acceptable for men since the outbreak of war. Now it was acceptable for women too, though nice girls did not smoke in the street. An order was placed for 50,000 book matches for use in the Soda Fountain and at the Tobacco Counter.

A new species of employee made her appearance in the 1920s - the store policewoman. Early in the decade, a Miss O'Neill was hired by Switzers, shared with Brown Thomas and other Grafton Street shops at a cost of 15s. a week, which the Board considered very good value.

Top: *The American influence was very strong.*
Left: *Enjoying a smoke in public.*
Opposite top: *The new expanded Switzers, 1927.*
Far right: *Children's fashion, 1924.*
Right: *A section of the Times Library in Switzers.*

Pilfering was beginning to be a problem. Advice was sought from the Times Library Service in London about the stealing of books from the library. Subscriptions of pilferers should be suspended, they were told. In 1924, Miss O'Neill had her first cases apprehended in Switzers. A Mrs Dunne was fined £1 for shoplifting and a nurse from the Rotunda was placed in the hands of the police.

In the Twenties, sales tended to see-saw between sudden downturns, causing concern and discussions with buyers on new methods for "forcing trade", and upswings, when staff were awarded bonuses and increases in salaries.

It was a time when a new balance was being negotiated in staff-employer relations. The Distributive Workers Union, representing all shop workers, replaced the Drapers' Assistants' Association and there were several confrontations between union and managements. Negotiations were often difficult for men used to the deferences and unquestioned hierarchies of an earlier age but new relationships and new ways of treating claims were steadily established.

Trade was sufficiently healthy in 1927 and the future promising enough for Switzers to invest in a new acquisition. Johnsons Diamond Merchants at 94 Grafton Street, on the corner of Wicklow Street, was bought out - premises and stock - for £20, 000. Switzers now stretched along the entire block and was joined with its premises in Wicklow Street.

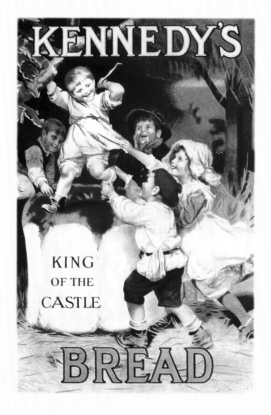

In the 1920s and early 1930s, decades devoted to the concept of progress and modernity, Brown Thomas cultivated an identity similar to Selfridges of London. The shop's motto might equally have been "Spend The Day At Brown Thomas". Women were invited to make use of the Writing Room. "We want you to make it your Club - it's an ideal spot for meeting your friends, reading the news of the day or writing your letters". The Writing Room was "a delightfully comfortable rendezvous, ideal for a chat, a read or letter writing…"

They could attend a beauty lecture, or one of the daily Juventa demonstrations where one learned how to make the most of one's attractive features with the use of cosmetics.

While mother wrote letters or gossiped or learned beauty secrets, the children could attend a Juvenile Mannequin Parade and then be further entertained by watching "the interesting Cinematograph Films on the Kodascope, especially arranged for children courtesy of Kodak Ltd."

In the Portrait Studio, you could have your photograph taken and go home with "a large beautifully finished print for the very moderate sum of 2/11". Or inspect the new Atwater Kent radiogram. All this and manage to buy a "Fifty shilling coat" as well. "Amazing value", cried the advertisements.

Top Left: *An example of advertising art-work from the period.*
Left: *Juvenile mannequin parades held regularly at Brown Thomas.*
Opposite Top: *Dublin's prettiest girl, Miss Eileen Ryan.*
Opposite Right: *"Pat Rooney" by Pat Rooney.*

From 1926 Harry Selfridge's son, Harry Selfridge Junior, was Managing Director of the Selfridge subsidiary, Selfridges Provincial Stores Ltd. of which Brown Thomas was one. On one of the two lions couchant over the great doors of Selfridges, the likeness of his face was said to be carved, and his father's on the other.

At Brown Thomas in the early '30s, there were the new American modes, full of "chic" and "snap". Of "transatlantic breeziness and vivacity you're going to fall in love with…" Stockings were still silk - grenadine silk, pleated silk and lisle, silk wool marl, "the very thing for sports and country wear, to blend with the new tweeds".

A new type of woman had now been identified, the "business girl". Special mannequin parades were arranged, of interest to the business girl, and to suit her lifestyle, at 5.30 in the evening. Their object was to "demonstrate most effectively just how simple it is for the business girl to dress tastefully and at moderate cost". The parades were compered by Miss Dorothy Nevin, the thoroughly fun and French fashion commentator, said to be "a delightful actress" as well as a good saleswoman.

Aquiline features and the tall wide-shouldered silhouette was in vogue, replacing the perky flapper girl of a few years before. Miss Nevin claimed to be in possession of the secret of how to appear inches taller than you really were and promised to divulge it during her commentary. Evening gowns were of silk crêpe de chine, were longer and flared out from the knee; hats were small and worn at a rakish angle over the right eye…

At the Theatre Royal in 1933, Dublin's prettiest girl was judged to be Miss Eileen Ryan. Miss Ryan was presented with an evening gown made by Brown Thomas and was then engaged to model furs for them during the Fur Sale. At the same time, Pat Rooney, the eminent Fleet Street Cartoonist, held a salon in the shop. From Mr Rooney, you could have "a clever cartoon of yourself" - 2/6 - or your "pet tail-wagger" - 5s.

In December 1933, Harry Selfridge Junior made a surprise announcement. Selfridges was disposing of its Irish store to "Irish interests". The sale, Harry Junior explained, was due to business conditions in the Irish Free State "becoming steadily less good in recent years".

In fact, the effects of the Depression were not felt in Ireland until 1933. The real reason, understandably evaded by Harry Junior, was that his father was financially pressed and was selling off his peripheral assets. Indeed, it was soon clear that he was broke. As well as building expensive additions to his London store and buying a string of shops in the provinces, among them Brown Thomas in Dublin, he had been having a splendid time in the Roaring Twenties.

Always improvident and high-spending - he is said to have gone through three fortunes - he became an extravagant patron of the Dolly sisters - actresses - and treated them to an endless round of sprees, parties and balls. He was a keen gambler. A few days before the Derby in 1929, he rashly bought a fancied horse, PDQ, for a high price. PDQ was unplaced.

The "Irish interests" referred to by Harry Selfridge Junior in his announcement about the sale of Brown Thomas in December 1933 were a man called John McGuire and his two sons, Edward and James. John McGuire was, in his own way, almost as spectacular a figure in the retail trade in Ireland as Selfridge had been abroad.

One of the new ascendancy, the Catholic middle-class, John McGuire was a native of Waterford. Apprenticed to the drapery trade as a young man in Robertson, Ledlie and Co. on the Quays, he went on to become General Manager of Hearne and Co., a firm with modest beginnings but which in McGuire's time there, employed hundreds of staff. As well as selling drapery and household goods, Hearnes had a furniture and a church goods department.

In 1920, he moved to Dublin, turned the Shelbourne House on Merrion Row into a booming success and in 1923 was asked by Dr Lombard Murphy, the owner of Clerys on O'Connell Street, to take over its management. After the devastation of the Rising, Clerys had been rebuilt into a great store in the neo-classical style of Selfridges but was worryingly unprofitable.

The terms McGuire made with Clerys were unprecedentedly ambitious - £3000 a year and a substantial share in the profits. In his charge, Clerys became an enormous success. His style of management was firmly "hands-on" and he used glamorous advertising devices, of which aeroplanes were a central part. Indeed, he proved so successful and so expensive that Clerys' owners came to feel after ten years that he was expendable. On the 21st of November 1933, he was dismissed.

By early December, he had acquired the controlling interest in Selfridges' Irish store. As an employee, John McGuire had always been restive. The purchase of Brown Thomas gave him the opportunity to be a sole proprietor.

Top: *John F. McGuire, circa 1935.*
Right: *Always up-to-date, Brown Thomas stocked the latest in gramophones.*
Opposite: *Harry Selfridge signs Brown Thomas over to John F. McGuire, 1933.*

That Brown Thomas intended to compete with its nearest and most formidable rival, Switzers, was obvious at once. A new Hairdressing and Beauty Salon "equipped with the most modern fittings and under the direction of Monsieur Felix" opened in January. Soon Monsieur Felix was demonstrating the new Madison Wireless Permanent Wave, on a living model. "No machine is connected to the head and no electricity used on the hair - so you may walk around, telephone and generally amuse yourself while ensuring deep lustrous natural waves…"

The Modern Tea Room was opened, "designed in keeping with the new decorations in evidence all over the store". Here, you could have Dainty Afternoon Tea for 1/- to the strains of Miss Lucy Leenane's String Orchestra. During Fashion Week, live models wearing dresses of a design favoured by film-star Loretta Young walked to and fro for inspection by customers during their afternoon tea. A succession of Fashion Experts, Miss Vera Shepstone, Miss Evelyn Scarlett and Miss Jeanne Kent, gave lectures on How To Be Fashionable and on Colour Schemes to Suit Your Colouring.

Top: *Brown Thomas was always to the fore with modern fashion trends.* Top and Right: *A demonstration of the Madison Wireless Permanent Wave.*

Madame Booker, the Expert Corsetiere, was regularly in attendance. Her newest style in the late '30s was a garment called the Radio-Active Corset. Radio-activity was obviously still considered progressive and a good thing although the implication of plutonium nuggets nestling busily in the corset's bones was almost definitely metaphorical.

The McGuires cultivated a modern, friendly and personalised approach. Photographs of Buyers with their personal statements alongside were featured in advertisements - Mr Stark in Haberdashery, Jewellery, Perfumery and Umbrellas, Mr Coffey, buyer of Sheets and Table Linens, Mr Martin, Silks and Dress Materials. At a time when women still almost invariably left work on marriage, there were very few women Buyers - although there was Miss Moppett, Buyer of Ladies Model Gowns, Coats and Frocks.

Above: *Radioactive corset.*
Left: *Miss Scarlett during one of her popular "Fashion talks".*

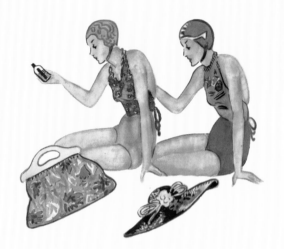

In 1934, new synthetic materials made their first appearance. "Tenniseene - the new fabric made from soft artificial silk - for the loveliest white tennis and sports frocks". Siltex was another. And in 1934 a chic young lady was shown in bell-bottom trousers at the "Exciting new Cruising and Beach Exhibition in the Fabric Hall".

Coco Chanel had invented the fashionable pursuit of the Tan. Sun Tan lotions and creams could be had at the Perfumery counter - under Miss Una Thompson. The "super-soft pure wool Bathing Costumes" in black, navy, green and maroon were soon giving way to sleeker backless styles in Mediterranean colours of red and turquoise blue.

A new Electrical Home Equipment Department opened, selling Electric Cookers, Refrigerators and every Modern Appliance for Washing, Cleaning and Ironing.

A fleet of new Delivery Vans daily served houses as far as Bray, Foxrock and Howth and porters were told to make full use of them and not to despatch parcels by post - "as our customers prefer to receive their purchases by means of our vans". The sight of a Brown Thomas delivery van drawing up at one's gate was becoming a source of prestige and pride in far-flung suburbs.

Top: *"Accessories are most important this summer".*

In the middle of these developments, a smart contemporary commentator, B.B. from *The Standard*, paid a visit to Brown Thomas.

"The place was bright with Shannon juice", she wrote. "Brilliant lights showed up the glitter and colour of womens' weaknesses…The store was gay, it was alive, it was smiling. Then I remembered that Mr McGuire was now in charge…"

What really gripped B. B. was "the array of the daintiest flowered muslin aprons which would make any modern maid stay at least six months in each place". The "servant problem" was one Brown Thomas customers were clearly familiar with.

"No maid could drop the tea-tray whilst wearing one of these aprons, they are too dainty and fairy-like and they are to be had for the positively elfin price of 2/6".

Above: *Newspaper advertisement "3 great offers in Maids' Dainty Aprons…"*

Far Left: *"Beachwear and cruising ideas".*
Middle: *"Everything under the sun at Brown Thomas".*
Left: *"Step into Beachwear like these from Brown Thomas … The Kippy Swim Suit, The Jantzen, and Beachrobes in stripes of red, green, orange and blue".*

FOR CONVENTS
BROWN THOMAS

Brown Thomas for samples. We keep everything *ts at keenest prices*		BARGAIN IN NUNS' VEILING FAST DYED
ds, 3/5 dozen 3/6 dozen ck Worsted Reels, ozen.	Coloured Wool Mending Balls **40/- gross.** Gold Polonaise, for Linings 36 inches wide. **4/6** a yard. Berry and Mulberry Pins, **16/6** gross.	40 inches wide **3/9** yard Usually 4/11 a yard ASK FOR A SAMPLE OF THIS
BON AINS	BARGAINS IN Pure Wool FLANNEL	A GREAT BARGAIN IN BLACK SERGE

Brown Thomas was assuming an identity that contemporaries might have described as "toney". An Exhibition of Modern Paintings in the Tea-Room was the beginning of what was later to become an art gallery in the new basement. The first show, of the École De Paris, included works by Andre Derain, Andre Lhote, the Irish painter Doreen Vanston de Padilla, and Henri Hayden, a Cubist painter later to become an intimate friend of Samuel Beckett.

But John McGuire was an astute businessman who continued to cultivate the goodwill of customers from all walks of life. Clerys, his former shop, did an excellent trade in clerical outfitting and he saw no reason why Brown Thomas too should not enjoy the favour of the religious orders. This was the heyday of the convent, when almost every town had a large and thriving community of nuns at the centre of its school and hospital system. In these pre-Vatican Council days, nuns still wore medieval-style habits and had very particular requirements.

Soon, he was writing to Reverend Mothers up and down the country.

"Dear Reverend Madam,
I have the pleasure to announce that I have purchased from Selfridges, London, their entire interests in Brown Thomas of Grafton St. Dublin…

I intend to cater for convent requirements and will carry full stocks of everything that convents and hospitals require, the same as I did in Clerys. I shall be grateful for some of your orders, which I shall try to deserve by offering as good or better value than anyone else…"

Top: *Painter preparing for his forthcoming exhibition at Brown Thomas.*
Left: *In the 1930s, nuns and priests became a whole new market for Brown Thomas.*

To 500 convents throughout Ireland he forwarded a coloured poster advertising the interesting bargains to be had at Brown Thomas.

"Best American Pyalin for Guimps; Virgin Blue Cloaking for Children of Mary; Brussels Nets for Veils; Black Serge; Scapular Braids, Red, Blue and Brown; Nuns' Comfortable Seamless Shoes…"

While John McGuire was the shrewd business brain behind Brown Thomas, it was his son and fellow Director, Edward McGuire, who was entrusted with its aesthetic appeal.

Ned, as he was known, was a man of many parts. An all-round athlete, he also painted, and was a star of lawn-tennis. For ten seasons, 1924-35, he represented Ireland in the Davis Cup, won the Open and Close Singles Championships of Ireland in 1931, was twice Hard Court Champion, and several times shared in Irish Doubles titles. He would later be appointed a Director of the National Gallery and a Senator of the Irish Free State.

Within a generation the McGuires had been transformed from country drapers into the aristocracy of the Free State.

At Brown Thomas, Ned's father gave him a free hand to realise a long-cherished desire - to create a beautiful store. Ned saw no reason why aesthetic and commercial considerations should be incompatible or why inexpensive things should be regarded as aesthetically unattractive. It was he who gave Brown Thomas its rejuvenated image as a centre of international style and fashion.

Top: "Good shot, Ned!"
Right: The McGuire coat of arms.

He was especially interested in design and display.
Classical columns replaced the iron props which supported
the ceilings. Most of the plasterwork required for the
columns and the new balustrade around the balcony was
made in the store from wax moulds by a plasterer who was
part of the maintenance team. A new principal staircase of
marble in an Italian classical design was installed and in the
general decorative features around the store, a classical
theme was dominant.

His cleverest innovation perhaps was the employment of a
friend of his, the painter Norah McGuinness, to design the
window displays. Norah was a young modernist painter of
considerable reputation who had worked in Paris under
Andre Lhote. Well-travelled – she spent the mid '30s in
India and Egypt – she lived too for a time in New York.

Travelling on a bus up Fifth Avenue one day, she observed
a furious Salvador Dali being ejected from a department
store by a policeman. Dali, incensed by the objections of
customers to his window display of a fur-lined bath, had
attempted to throw the bath through the glass onto the
pavement.

This inspired Norah to design windows herself and she worked for some of New York's most prominent department stores, including Lord & Taylors. She returned to Ireland just before the Second World War and during her long career juggled her work as a painter with commercial design and illustration.

Though prominent in the avant garde of the art world - she was chairman of the Living Art Exhibition's committee for some decades and represented Ireland in the Venice Biennale of 1950 - Norah McGuinness immediately accepted Ned McGuire's invitation in the early '40s to design displays for his shop. She had originally trained as an illustrator, had worked as a designer for the Abbey Theatre, illustrated books by Maria Edgeworth, W.B. Yeats and Elizabeth Bowen, and had worked with Vogue in London.

Even under the Selfridges, Brown Thomas had not enjoyed the services of a display artist. Windows were still a confusion of hundreds of articles, with as many departments and buyers represented as there was available space.

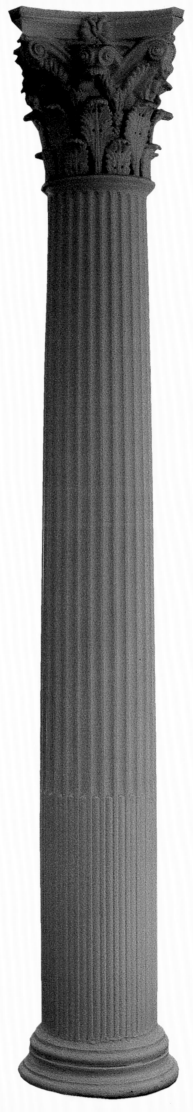

Left: *Norah McGuinness circa 1947.*
Right and Far Left: *Classical columns were a McGuire innovation, as was the idea of using window displays.*
Opposite: *An early window display by Norah McGuinness.*

Norah McGuinness saw that a window should have, as she put it, "a motif".

"You had to have a motif. The article might be only a pair of gloves, but you would make a picture around them. It extends the message of the merchandise. It makes clear to the customer what the shop is like, what class of goods they can buy there".

For a week in Spring, Ned McGuire turned Norah loose on the windows in Grafton Street. What she did to them stopped the traffic, literally, it is said.

"No one had ever seen anything like it before. I made the window more like a stage set - painting a picture, telling a tale of Spring. It was such a success that he told me to do it again in the Autumn".

Soon she was employed at Brown Thomas on a full-time basis and even in the late 1960s (when she was in her sixties) she was working there three days a week and painting Cubist inspired pictures in her studio on the other three.

There was a great deal of window space to be filled. Until the '70s Brown Thomas still had its Victorian-style Arcade along Grafton Street. Behind the facade with its shallow display area ran a passage with another set of windows opening on to the shop interior, creating for Norah's purposes a sort of walk-in theatre set. The Brown Thomas Arcade was also a well-known meeting-place, as popular for southsiders as Clerys clock was for northsiders.

In the 1940s, an apprentice, Jimmy O'Raw, came to work with Norah and found himself "on a constant roll of excitement" from the challenging preparations for her Christmas shows to the Sales, the Spring collections and the big fashion shows twice a year. One year during the '50s she painted the window-sets black. It looked wonderful and started a trend. She became very interested in lighting effects and was the first to use pinhead, spot and flood lights.

In December 1943, when the McGuire's tenure of Brown Thomas was exactly ten years old, the staff, as a mark of their appreciation and affection, made a presentation to their popular Chairman and Managing Director, John F.

Fashionable portraitist Leo Whelan was commissioned to paint Mr McGuire's portrait for a fee of one hundred and fifty guineas.

The finished work was presented to him on Friday the 10th at a dinner in the Hibernian Hotel. Two hundred and ten people sat down to table. A Waterford woman and leading member of staff, Mrs Peggy Hartnett, presented Mr McGuire with his portrait.

Then a merry evening was had by all, as members of staff such as Miss Fulham, Mr Reddin, Mr Lecky and Miss O'Keefe, entertained the guests with recitations, songs, and violin, piano and whistling solos.

Top: *John F. McGuire with Miss Peggy Hartnett.*
Left: *Presentation dinner, Hibernian Hotel, December 10th 1943.*
Opposite Top: *A crowd-stopping window display by Norah McGuinness*
Opposite Bottom: *Norah in action.*

In 1942 it was the turn of Management to take to the streets in protest.

It was the middle of the Second World War, known in determinedly neutral Ireland as The Emergency. Uninvolved with the war effort, the Emergency was experienced largely as a stagnant period of inactivity and suspension, with blackouts, limitations on travel and rationing of imported goods like petrol, tea and sugar.

When the rationing of clothing was being considered by the Government, the drapers' unions urged managements to demonstrate against the measure. Ronald Nesbitt, manager of Arnotts, remembers walking bashfully from Parnell Street to Leinster House between the bulky figure of Denis Guiney of Clerys and the elegant one of Edward McGuire, representing Brown Thomas.

The demonstration did not bring about the desired result and clothing was rationed. The drapery trade was further put out when, to save on materials, controlled yardages and styles were specified for different garments. Skirts were shortened, pleats were frowned upon and any unnecessary tucks or folds were disallowed. The more recondite arts of the dressmaker fell into disuse. They were plain clothes for plain times. In tune with a general atmosphere of austerity, one newspaper, *The Irish Independent*, refused to carry advertisements for corsets in which the model's legs were visible!

With the shortage of goods, the tailors and tailoresses in the workshops were kept especially busy with alterations and repairs. There was an elderly man who renovated handbags. "You gave him your old handbag and he returned it to you like new", says Maire Mac An tSaoi. She was now "a tied customer" of Brown Thomas as her mother had given her an account of her own there and she would never have thought of going anywhere else.

Above: *"Censorship" during the "Emergency".*

Eamonn MacThomais, who started work in Switzers as a messenger boy just before the war, had been promoted to the position of the Kingstown Boy. He was the boy on Switzers' most important delivery van, the one that served the Dun Laoghaire district - a town still loyally called Kingstown in Switzers. Because petrol was rationed, the van ran on charcoal and Eamonn was supplied with two pairs of overalls, one to stoke the fire, and one to wear when making his deliveries. There were also vans which carried large gas balloons on their roofs. Customers on the Kingstown route tended to be especially illustrious. The great tenor, Count John McCormack was one; another was Lord Meath of Bray who was intrigued by the charcoal-driven van.

During the Emergency, wage increases were modest due to the Standstill Order of 1941. Sales remained buoyant however. Brown Thomas had the basement excavated, giving a great amount of extra space and the Little Theatre, used mainly as an art gallery, opened there.

Maire Mac An tSaoi remembers Brown Thomas as the "artistic mecca" of Dublin during the war years. The Modern Tea Rooms were a meeting-place not just for ladies who shopped but also for intellectuals and artists. The young Maire liked its ambience too because it was frequented by young men! The poet and Director of the National Gallery, Thomas McGreevy, was often to be been seen there.

Above: *"Power dressing for the Forties"*.

With the ending of the Emergency in 1945, Grafton Street was thronged with euphoric crowds. Students at Trinity hung out the Union Jack and were rumoured to have burnt the tricolour in a show of contempt at Ireland's neutrality. The ribbon counter in Switzers, wrote Eamonn MacThomais, did a roaring trade — "One end of it was selling red white and blue ribbon and the other end was selling green white and orange ribbon". Miss Roberts in Switzers Fur Department produced the largest box of chocolates that a young sweet-starved apprentice, Nita Boylan, had ever seen. There were bonuses for employees and a boom in trade when the pent-up spending impulse could at last be satisfied and when English consumers, after long years of frugality, crossed the sea to luxuriate in the pleasure of buying in the well-stocked stores of Dublin.

For the first Christmas after the War, Norah McGuinness, perhaps expressing Ireland's sense of remoteness from it and a certain wistful nostalgia now that it was over, gave the Toy Fair a war theme. There were guns, tanks, bomber aircraft and camouflage outfits, and an intricate spider's web made from string in the Stock Room in front of each display. The kids – and many of their parents – loved it!

Above: *Dubliners breathed a sigh of relief at the end of World War II and Brown Thomas caught the mood of optimism in its Christmas Toy Fair, 1945.*

Christian Dior created his enormously popular "New Look' in 1947, long ballerina skirts that used a profligate amount of material. After the severely cut, unadorned Emergency style, the New Look seemed extravagantly graceful and feminine.

Brown Thomas opened its Dior Boutique in 1950, in the gallery later to be the outlet for the well-known Irish designer, Paul Costelloe. Brainchild of Edward McGuire, it was a replica of the Dior Salon in Paris, painted a subtle pastel grey with white trim. Monsieur and Madame Dubarry, known as "the explosive French couple" because of their fiery temperaments, handpainted a frieze of fleur de lys, scrolls and spirals around the door and the bow window that looked into the Damask Tea Rooms.

Dior himself came over for the opening, bringing his own models with him. One of them, a Swedish beauty called Brigitta, would marry John McGuire, Edward's son, and heir-apparent to Brown Thomas - another son, Edward junior, would become a renowned painter and portraitist. In the tea-room, and fitted out with gilt chairs with red plush seats, an elegant Dior dress, changed every day, was displayed.

Above: *"The Dior look"*.
Left: *Mrs Brigitta McGuire.*

In 1947, *The Drapers' Assistant,* still in existence, was again making hostile references to Switzers, and especially to Mr McQuiston, the Managing Director, late of Harrods. Unlike the family-run Brown Thomas, Switzers was a public company, with, inevitably, a somewhat more impersonal approach. A Mr William Hastings, newly employed in the Men's Outfitting Department, was at the centre of a row that ended after a nine and a half weeks strike.

The Union took issue with Switzers because Mr Hastings, on arriving at Switzers, an "organised house", applied for union membership. As he had previously been employed for twelve years at Grandys Gents' Outfitters on Stephen's Green and was only now applying for membership, the Union took this to mean that Switzers were willing to employ non-unionised staff. The custom was that an organised house should not employ anyone with less than six months Union membership. The Union therefore demanded that the services of Mr Hastings should be dispensed with.

Management resolved not to give way. For nine and a half weeks, Switzers was closed as staff picketed the premises and *The Drapers' Assistant* discoursed on the iniquities of management. "They are employing whom they like… Switzers is the only House with this problem… In the last ten years, ten male apprentices have been let go by them on completion of their apprenticeships.… "

It was bitterly cold weather with snow and frost. Picketers froze as they wound their way monotonously around Grafton Street and Wicklow Street. But there was some fun to be had. Passing customers took pity on them and used to invite their "girls" over to the Wicklow Hotel for a warming cup or "a drop of the craythur". The picketers made slides along Wicklow Street and skated on the frozen pond in Stephen's Green.

Two young apprentices, Edna Deacon and Nita Boylan, were agreeably surprised to find that they were earning more on the picket-lines than as workers. There was a uniform strike pay for everyone and they got £1 instead of the 14/3 they got in wages after a 9d. contribution for National Health.

Management stuck to its guns. The strike was settled with a Union card for Mr Hastings. After six months suspension on full pay he took up his position at Switzers. In return, the Union won a promise from the Federated Union of Employers that they would consider a wage claim. But Miss Hamilton Reid, later a Chairman of Switzers, has said the strike was the greatest upheaval the shop ever had to face. Nita Boylan remembers that for a long time, the climate of mutual trust and loyalty in the shop was not the same as before, that an animosity had been built up between management and staff.

In the following year, 1948, Brown Thomas celebrated its centenary. Unquestioned loyalty on the part of staff was universally considered in the trade as essential to a store's success. There was a saying - "Good and loyal staff can sell sand to an Arab". At the Centenary Dance in the Shelbourne, the McGuires were reassured, if they were in any doubt, of the absolute loyalty and devotion of their employees.

Bruce Martin, on behalf of staff, spoke with warmth and touching sincerity of the high esteem in which the Chairman and his family were held. John F. McGuire was presented with an Illuminated Address to mark the Centenary of "this famous and fashionable Grafton Street Store". "Your precept and example", said Mr Martin, "has been like a torch to show the way to higher ideals to make life happier and better for us all".

"We are more than just members of a business community or employees of an up-to-date Store", he continued, "but rather form part of a large family circle of which you are the Head. We all feel and realise you take a deep and personal interest in our joys and sorrows, in sickness you visit and comfort us, and when we get married, the Bridal Gift is never forgotten. It may truly be said, the sons and daughters of this house 'shall arise and call you blessed'…"

For the Chairman's wife, Mrs McGuire, there was a Lizard Skin Handbag. "Your gentle ways", said Mr Martin, "have endeared you to us all, and as you pass in and out amongst us, the smile and kind words are never forgotten". He then read two verses from Byron's "She Walks In Beauty", declaring that he thought them "very applicable to you".

To Ned McGuire, recently elected to the Senate, two Sixteenth Century Table Lamps were presented. Mr Martin made graceful remarks about the Senator's intellectual gifts and other qualities. "In the world of Art, you are not only a patron but have made a special study of the Fine Arts and have the Artist's eye to discern the beautiful in Architecture".

Above: *Senator McGuire at the National Gallery, circa 1990.*
Opposite Top: *Mr Hickey, Company Secretary, Brown Thomas.*
Opposite: *Switzers staff relax after bringing in the harvest.*

There was a touch of levity in the presentation to Mr
Hickey, Company Secretary, of an Engraved Silver Cigarette
Box. Mr Hickey was a bachelor and Mr Martin hoped that
the cigarette box would be a constant reminder to him that
he would now be required "to strike matches - or should I
have said a match - coming in so close contact with the fair
sex every day". Mr Martin declared he really didn't know
how Mr Hickey had escaped so long and regretted that on
this occasion "I have not to make a Presentation to Mrs
Hickey".

The spirit of loyalty was not confined to the shop. In the
very wet summer of 1946 the harvest was threatened and
shop assistants volunteered to help. Management co-
operated by giving them days off, staff gave their Sundays,
and for two or three weeks they worked in the fields.

Nita Boylan from Switzers remembers going in a cheerful
gang up to Cavendish House, headquarters of the Drapers'
Assistants' Association. Baskets of tea and sandwiches were
distributed by the Union and then they travelled out to the
countryside around Newcastle by lorry. It was a long way
from the scented halls of Grafton Street - but, according to
Nita, "mighty craic".

As the finest shops on Dublin's finest shopping street, a position in Switzers or Brown Thomas was sought after. Edna Deacon remembers that there were "books of names" seeking apprenticeships when she was granted an interview at Switzers in the '40s.

She paraded up and down before Mr McQuiston, who considered whether her deportment and looks fulfilled Switzers' criteria. Edna regarded Switzers as "the store" and knew that Switzers girls were renowned for their beauty. She passed the test, her mother agreed to pay her apprenticeship fee of £50 and she was in. For three years, she served her time, spending six months in each department; starting as a "duster", moving on to Stationery, Delivery and then to the Workrooms where, as a "runner", she carried garments up and down from the shop for alteration.

Sylvia Herron was bolder. She was a sixteen year old dropout from school when she wandered into Brown Thomas and was filled with awe. She took one look at the spiral staircase, leading up to the workrooms and knew she had to work there. She thought it was the most romantic place she had ever seen, pervaded with heady scents from the Cosmetics Department and with fresh flowers massed everywhere.

Next day, dressed in her elder sister's black suit and a little beret perched on her head, she arrived and asked to see the Manager. Informed that an apprenticeship fee would be required, she told him that her mammy was sick and her daddy unemployed. Christmas was near. Sylvia was taken on for three weeks in the Toy Department and put in charge of Dolls Clothes - "There were hundreds of them. Small, medium and large…."

Above: *There was great competition for jobs at Switzers, as Sylvia Herron recalls.*

After Christmas, she asked if she could be kept on. She had obviously shown potential as a saleslady and was given an apprenticeship in the China Department. The fee was waived. Sylvia spent twenty years at Brown Thomas in a chequered career of rapid promotions and demotions. Irrepressible high spirits, outspokenness and bad timekeeping saw her mounting the stairs to the Manager's office on a regular basis.

The customer, who of course was always right, could make inordinate demands. An American lady wanted a plaque in her family name of Murphy.

"Can you translate it into Gaelic?" she asked Sylvia. And Sylvia could, because she was able to read it off the back.

"Murchú", she recited perfectly.
But the customer wanted more.

"Can you translate it into Latin?" she asked.

"If I could do that", retorted Sylvia, "'tis down in Trinity College I'd be".

Soon she was making her way up those stairs again. She had been "politely impertinent", the customer reported.

Above and Left: Fifties fashion.

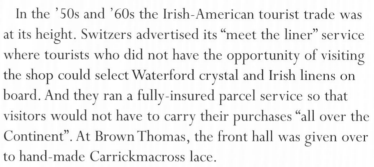

In the '50s and '60s the Irish-American tourist trade was at its height. Switzers advertised its "meet the liner" service where tourists who did not have the opportunity of visiting the shop could select Waterford crystal and Irish linens on board. And they ran a fully-insured parcel service so that visitors would not have to carry their purchases "all over the Continent". At Brown Thomas, the front hall was given over to hand-made Carrickmacross lace.

In the China Department, Sylvia Herron found a strict ranking system operating among the salespersons - a practice disapproved of by Management but favoured by senior staff because of the potential for commission. A junior like Sylvia, ranked Number Five, was hardly allowed to serve at all. Customers too were graded according to their potential spending power. When a likely-looking grade one customer appeared in the Department, saleslady number one called "Forward Number One" and stepped out to greet her.

One day when business was brisk, a very rakish and scruffy looking gentleman rambled in.

"Forward Number Five", sniffed the senior assistant.

The scruffy gentleman, as it turned out, was the Editor of the *New York Herald Tribune* and he wanted suites of both Waterford and Lismore glass, with twelve of everything. It was an unprecedented coup for Sylvia. The commission would be large.

Half-way through the transaction, Number One stepped in.

"I'll take over now", she smiled sweetly.

"Get away from me", hissed Sylvia.

"I would like this young lady to serve me", interjected the New York gentleman.

Number One was obliged to withdraw. Later she attacked Sylvia with a feather duster.

Edna Deacon, who was now Cosmetics Buyer at Brown
Thomas and was introducing exclusive lines like Estée
Lauder, Guerlain and Erno Laszlo, remembers how
employees were imbued with a sense of "the honour and
glory" of being there. Wages were not high and a pension
scheme had only lately been introduced. But every staff
member felt highly valued all the same.

Senator McGuire arrived at the shop every morning at ten
minutes to nine, "beautifully groomed", in a show of
solidarity and example. At Christmas he presented lady
assistants with a carnation and a personal greetings card. The
male assistants got tobacco. At the annual Fashion Ball in the
Gresham where there was a dance programme of Foxtrots,
Quicksteps and Waltzes, the copious champagne was
provided by the Senator.

Staff were required to be exemplars of the grace and
elegance that was Brown Thomas's identity. Until the '70s,
lady assistants had to wear a hat and gloves to work. Sylvia
Herron used to carry her hat in her hand and pop it on her
head just as she entered the shop.

Uniforms varied from decade to decade and according to
changing fashions. In the '50s, Senator McGuire noted that
some assistants were wearing "revealing" blouses and
instituted a regime of grey dresses, flannel for Summer,
wool for Winter. Later they became Crimplene and pastel.
A Miss McNamara - known as Nellie Mac, was the last
assistant over in Switzers, to wear the long black silk skirt
introduced before the First World War.

Right: *The "beautifully groomed"*
Senator Ned McGuire.
Opposite: *Just one of the many*
amusing incidents involving the
mischievous Sylvia Herron.

Every morning at 8.30, the Commissionaires of Switzers and Brown Thomas could be seen polishing the brasswork on the entrance doors of their respective shops. By 9.30, they would be positioned in full regalia -coat or jacket with well-polished brass buttons, knife-edged trousers, cap with its shining leather peak, and gloves, to greet customers alighting from cars, fetch them taxis and ensure that no "undesirables" were allowed to loiter in or around the entrances. Customers too were equally well-groomed. Matching gloves, shoes and handbag were essential accessories for the well-dressed woman. After having chosen a bag, seated comfortably by the handbag counter and ably advised by the assistant, she was escorted to the ladies footwear department, introduced and handed over to the care of a saleslady apprised of her requirements. At the front and back of the store were two high desks, connected by Lamson tubes to the cash office to where she was graciously escorted once appropriately accoutred.

Customers often had favoured assistants in the various departments to whom they referred as "my girl in Brown Thomas" or "my man in Switzers". At the beginning of November, they would come in with their Christmas list and, seated comfortably, would go through it with their favourite assistant. Often, having specified possible items and the amount they wanted to spend, the list would be entrusted entirely to "Miss Boylan" or "Miss Deacon".

Even the most indulged customers were not privy however to "Ben Lang". This was a Drapery Language, a lingo all of its own that had evolved through generations of drapery assistants, and was, naturally, wholly verbal. It was universal among all the drapery stores and so convenient to use in the hearing of an unsuspecting customer that some assistants conversed in nothing else.

"I dermont nermo".

"Lermuck ermat the kermiss of dermat".

"We'll germut nermuttin to germut hermur".

"Jermeezus kermist".

"Fermur kermoat and nermo ner micker".

Let it be enough to say that the first phrase means "I don't know" and the last is very rude!

Steadily however, old ways were dying out.
Apprenticeships in Brown Thomas ceased in 1950. The last
apprentice in Switzers, Gerry Walker, was indentured in
1956. The year before, Tommy Beatty, aged 15 was
indentured on the strength of letters of recommendation
from his Uncle Billy who had a cake-shop in South William
Street and from his local priest.

Even the youngest messenger or "duster" was expected to
wear a smart dark suit and white shirt. One of Tommy's first
jobs was to parcel the books from the Times Library for
delivery by van. One day a young delivery boy returned to
the department in a state of embarrassment. At a house
where he found nobody was at home, he had dropped the
book through an open window - and straight into the fish-
tank!

In 1958 the Times Library in London closed and a Switzers
van went out to Greystones with a book delivery for the last
time.

Left: *Brown Thomas
delivery boys would go to
great lengths to make
their deliveries.*

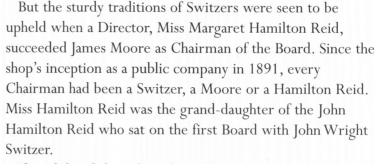

But the sturdy traditions of Switzers were seen to be upheld when a Director, Miss Margaret Hamilton Reid, succeeded James Moore as Chairman of the Board. Since the shop's inception as a public company in 1891, every Chairman had been a Switzer, a Moore or a Hamilton Reid. Miss Hamilton Reid was the grand-daughter of the John Hamilton Reid who sat on the first Board with John Wright Switzer.

Though her father, also John - whom she remembers having his morning pipe-smoke in the garden in Rathgar before taking the tram into Switzers - had died when she was two, she was always deeply involved with Switzers. Even as a schoolgirl, she had taken time off to attend their Annual General Meetings.

Miss Hamilton Reid saw in her role as Chairman a duty to uphold the shop's traditional policy of integrity. One tenet of this policy was never to stock anything which might be "detrimental to humankind". This was why Switzers never sold liquor or wine in its restaurants.

Another was its attitude to Sales - so that the slogan of long-standing, "Switzers, The Sale You Know Is Genuine", was entirely truthful. Switzers never departed from offering in its Sales only old stock at a reduced price, clearly-marked Seconds, and Special Offers. This included the manufacture of slow-selling fabrics and colours into garments, always by local factories, and priced accordingly. Miss Hamilton Reid had strong convictions about encouraging Irish industry.

Grafton Street in the 1950s.
Opposite: *The daring Flick Buckley "sparks" a great deal of interest in the Mary Quant collection.*

In 1959, the General Manager, Mr McQuiston retired and
was replaced by James Chapman, who had been previously
with several London stores, such as Harrods and Selfridges.
Under the affable, dapper Jimmy Chapman with his
handlebar moustache, Switzers was given a modern facelift
and re-organisation to meet the Swinging Sixties. The old-
fashioned mellow lighting was changed to simulate natural
lighting, the ornate display cabinets were replaced with
modern plate-glass and an airy sense of vastness and space
was evoked with a new decor. Glass, white wrought-iron
and climbing plants were used throughout to give an air of
freshness and modernity.

In the era of Beatlemania, the Record Rendezvous was an
essential venue for the hip among Dublin's youth. Here,
sound-proofed booths were provided to listen to the latest
singles. The affluent teenager could choose something off-
beat to wear at the Young And Gay Department before
meeting her friends for an espresso at Il Cappucino. The
Soda Fountain of the old days had vanished, now that Paris
was the hottest city and Juliette Greco's black polo-necks
the hippest look. Flick Buckley, the first Mary Quant
Consultant to Ireland, would dress every day in a daring
Quant mini and stroll, with her Quant badge, around the
store.

Switzers was in an expansionist phase. By the end of the decade, it had doubled its profits and become the Switzers Group. In 1962, it acquired Cashs in Cork - a deal completed by Harry Osman, Company Secretary, on the railway station platform when he topped up the Switzers offer with a half-crown. In 1963 Todds of Limerick was acquired; and in 1969, Moons of Galway, where King Edward had bought twelve Galway shawls on his motoring trip in 1907.

At the end of the decade, the magnificent French staircase that travelled up three floors and gave a panoramic view of the store was removed. Beautiful though it was, Miss Hamilton Reid was relieved to see it go. Unsupported, it bounced perceptibly when climbed and though it underwent a rigorous inspection by an architect before every Sale, she had always feared it could be a danger to the public. It is said that when the staircase was dismantled, it was "hanging by a string", proving Miss Hamilton Reid's fears well-founded.

In 1960, Brown Thomas won the Coupe D'Or Du Bon Gout Français for its good taste. In the following year, when Princess Grace, whose family was Irish-American, and her husband, Prince Rainier, visited Ireland, they stopped off at Brown Thomas.

Norah McGuinness, aided by Jimmy O'Raw, decorated the entire store in red and white, the Monaco colours. The columns were swagged in red and white, and cacti and other Mediterranean plants were imported especially. Staff were required to wear suits of Irish linen by Dorene in sunny sweetpea colours, lemon, peach, lilac. The Little Theatre had a photographic exhibition of Monaco's sights and an exhibition of arts and crafts from the Principality.

On the day itself, the shop was closed to the public. As the Princess's cavalcade drew up, Grafton Street was crowded with admirers. On the roof, Michael O'Reilly was perilously perched in readiness to haul down the Tricolour and hoist the Monaco flag once the royal couple had entered Brown Thomas.

Inside, the staff were lined up along the central aisle, the women in their pretty costumes, the men in tails. The line was headed by the Display Team so Norah McGuinness was the first to meet the Princess. It was agreed by all that Princess Grace was "utterly charming and exquisite" and that Prince Rainier had "stunning" blue eyes. The Princess was presented with a Carrickmacross lace mantilla and the mantilla immediately superseded the hat as demure headgear for Mass-going ladies.

Top: *Princess Grace and Prince Rainier arrive at Brown Thomas in 1961.*
Right: *Admiring crowds greet the Royal couple.*
Opposite: *The hanging French staircase in Switzers.*
Above Opposite: *Miss Hamilton Reid.*

Visiting stars of stage and screen of course always called to Grafton Street.

Movita, tiny, graceful and black-eyed and her tall, handsome, bejewelled husband, Jack Doyle, caused a sensation when they shopped in Switzers at the height of their fame in the '40s. Movita ordered a number of classic suits from the Tailoring Department and insisted that the buttons should be dyed to match the colour of each.

Edna Deacon was thrilled when James Mason looked with his "beautiful black eyes" into hers and asked to borrow her pencil… Ingrid Bergman was beautiful despite her unfashionable flat shoes and long black coat…

But Rita Hayworth who came in with Prince Ali Khan was a disappointment. She wore slacks and her gorgeous red hair was dull and nondescript. All the same, all the fellows rushed from every corner of the store to gaze upon her.

The theatrical Michéal MacLiammoir frequented both Switzers and Brown Thomas. The wife of a visiting African Prime Minister alighted from a chauffeur-driven car and bought only a surprisingly plentiful supply of men's undergarments…

With the new national television service, stars of the small screen became the faces to watch for; Gay Byrne, Cathal O'Shannon, Ronnie Walsh, Monica Sheridan were becoming household names. The Brown Thomas Men's Hairdresser, Tony Byrne, made a rather catastrophic appearance on the new controversial programme, the Late Late Show. He was asked to shave a man's head but his subject took fright half-way through and vanished.

Top: *John McGuire with the Ogham printed cloth commissioned by him from Irish Artists.*
Left: *The interior of Brown Thomas's Menswear Department, 1962.*

The new decade in 1970 brought changes to both Switzers and Brown Thomas. By the end of the '60s, spending, after a long spree and a rise in inflation, and therefore profits, had settled down and become static. The slippage was worrying and in 1971, Switzers finally submitted to ongoing pressure from takeover attempts, and was sold to Waterford Glass (headed by Patrick McGrath) and to a subsidiary of House of Fraser, which also owned Harrods in London. Miss Hamilton Reid, conscious of her long family tradition at Switzers, was reluctant to sell - "If I had had 51% of the equity, I wouldn't have sold". But, as a Director of Waterford Glass, she was able to maintain her interest in Switzers.

At Brown Thomas John McGuire brought in progressive "efficiency experts", time and motion people who engaged the staff in progressive selling techniques like role-playing. This did not catch on. In 1970, Brown Thomas was in troubled financial straits. There was talk of the store closing down. For a story about its imminent demise RTE cameras came to the store, to the consternation of the staff. A knight in shining armour, or at least with money in his pocket, was sorely needed.

He arrived, in the person of Galen Weston.

Galen Weston, though born in England, came from a close-knit Canadian Methodist family with a strong work ethic. He was a son, one of nine children, of Garfield Weston, the retailing and bakery magnate, based in Toronto. Garfield's father, George Weston, had founded the empire in 1882. It was Garfield who introduced wrapped loaves of bread to Britain in the '30s. Among the Weston properties was the famous London department store, Fortnum and Mason. By the '60s, the Weston empire included over 200 companies and subsidiaries across Northern America.

In the early '60s, Galen had completed his academic studies in Germany and England. He was sent to Northern Ireland to learn the trade from his father's friend, Jimmy Boyd, manager of a Weston holding, Stewart's supermarkets. Galen Weston was a questing young man keen to make his own mark in retailing. In 1963 he moved south of the border to Dublin, uncharted territory where the Weston empire was concerned.

He opened a shop called Food Fare at the back of Todco, formerly Todd Burns, owned by John McGuire, in Henry Street. Soon, he had started another shop which he called Powers. He chose the name because it was that of a supermarket in which he had worked as a boy in Canada and because he thought it suggested both energy and a sense of Irishness. Powers became a very successful supermarket chain which in the '70s was consolidated with Pat Quinn's Quinnsworth shops. He would in time create the enormously popular stores, Penneys, in Ireland.

Galen Weston had come to greatly love Ireland, its people and its culture. And in 1966 he married a top Irish model, Hilary Frayne. Hilary had often been seen on the ramp in the prestigious Brown Thomas Fashion Shows which were also showcases for Irish designers like Sybil Connolly, Wolfangel and Clodagh. The Westons settled down in a 17th century castle in Roundwood, Co. Wicklow, the former home of President Sean T. O'Kelly.

Top: *Galen Weston.*
Left: *Galen Weston (right) attending a Press conference with Pat Quinn.*

Hilary is often cited as the inspiration behind the Weston purchase of Brown Thomas at this crucial stage in its fortunes. She, like so many Dubliners, had a special attachment to Brown Thomas and wanted to see it continue to flourish. Her practical interest was made evident by her appointment as a Director in 1971. Her husband, for his part, was delighted to be able to acquire a store of such traditional quality and standing as Brown Thomas. His father was associated with Fortnum & Mason. He would be associated with Brown Thomas.

Within a few months of his acquisition, Galen Weston - described in a newspaper report as "a forceful and fast-moving" young man - also bought the Bailey in Duke Street. The Bailey was an old drinking and eating establishment, referred to in Joyce's "Ulysses" as Burtons. Latterly it had been owned by the painter and writer, John Ryan, who had acquired for its hallway the original door of number seven Eccles Street, home of Leopold Bloom. Under his management it had continued to be a favourite haunt of the more intellectual drinkers of the Grafton Street area. The Bailey now aimed to be as exclusive and glamorous as Brown Thomas was in the shop world. The pint was expensive, at 23p, but at the time its new seafood bar was one of the few in the city.

Winds of change, fresh and sometimes disturbingly bracing, were blowing through every aspect of Irish society in the 1970s. The age-worn hierarchies were rapidly collapsing. Ireland's new membership of the European Economic Community provided a great boost, economically and psychologically. Continental lifestyles and patterns of consumption were permeating Irish life. Well-educated young people, products of the baby boom of the '50s, impatient with the old order that they saw as out-dated, surged along the soon to be pedestrianised Grafton Street. Captain Americas, the first American-style burger restaurant on the street, was new and exciting.

Top: *The neo-Georgian windows, in the '60s.*
Middle: *The Bailey, Duke Street.*
Above: *Some advertising campaigns were more controversial than others.*

Marriage no longer obliged women to retire to the kitchen, and in the world of work and opportunity, they were steadily taking on new roles and responsibilities. Busy working women could not afford the time to shop in the old leisurely manner when a morning inspecting scarves or lingerie would be punctuated by a social visit to the Tea Rooms.

All this was bringing about a revolution in shopping. Self-service was now firmly established. The new chain stores which were arriving on Grafton Street encouraged the shopper to select freely from open displays, asking for advice only if she chose to do so. And they were making fashion accessible to everyone.

At Brown Thomas, the new ownership reflected the broader changes in Irish life. Galen and Hilary Weston were young, glamorous, forward-looking and international in their outlook. They wanted to retain Brown Thomas's reputation for quality and elegance but to give it an up-to-date character.

Galen Weston's first priority at Brown Thomas was to give it an immediate facelift and revitalise its merchandise. Galen was determined to develop a new direction for Brown Thomas which would secure its leadership long into the future. There followed a period of experimentation and reflection. The Hairdressing Salon was given a revamp in the style of an Oriental Garden, with greenery, wicker chairs and a butterfly motif. Wally Garland, who had cut Galen Weston's hair since Galen's arrival in Dublin, moved to Brown Thomas. The Damask Tea Rooms became the Social and Personal restaurant, serving the "new" fashionable foods like yoghurts and salads.

In 1972, Brown Thomas was the winner in the window display competition run by the Chamber of Commerce. Mrs. Maureen Lynch, wife of the Taoiseach Jack Lynch, presented the award to the Director Gerry Quinn who had come to Brown Thomas from Clerys with John F. McGuire in the 1930s. Norah McGuinness, now 67, retired. Her last Christmas display had a medieval theme with rich velvet swags everywhere and jousting poles. To replace her, the artistic and energetic "image maker", Ken Moore came from London.

Top: *Norah McGuinness shortly before she retired.*
Left: *Brown Thomas windows won many awards.*

Opposite Top: *Brown Thomas were stockists of the "supremely casual or rigidly formal", like this suit designed by Mark Russell.*
Opposite: *A model of Ken Moore's frontage for Brown Thomas.*

Working closely with Hilary Weston, in the years that
followed Ken developed an image that was fresh, classical
and elegantly distinctive. The neo-Georgian windows were
taken out and the Victorian style restored as they had been
in Hugh Brown's time. The Arcade was incorporated into the
shop, providing a greater sense of space. By 1978, nos 18-20
Grafton Street, formerly Lawrence's toy-shop and
Combridge's book and art supplies, were incorporated into
Brown Thomas and its proud new black frontage reached
the corner of Duke Street. Donough Callaghan, whose
saddlery had been on Dame Street since 1865 was invited to
occupy what had been Combridge's premises. His wooden
lifesize pony came with him ensuring that a new generation
of children would be fitted with a perfect size of jodhpurs.
The arrival of Callaghans also provided Brown Thomas with
a new insignia; the white horse's head that hung over the
door.

Managing Director Liam Walsh left to create a great success
of Gay Wear, the young fashion subsidiary of Brown Thomas
which went on to become the popular A-Wear. Cecily
McMenamin became Fashion Director and, for elegant
women, an independent arbiter of fashion.

Sylvia Herron's ebullience was now recognised as an asset - she had been appointed to the position of PRO. A very popular innovation was the introduction of the Food Hall. This huge delicatessen and grocery cast in the style of Fortnum & Mason occupied for a time the entire back of the store.

Larry Yourell was a young apprentice from Cabra who in the '70s was working in Lipton's grocery on Grafton Street. One of his tasks was to deliver bacon and ham to the Social and Personal restaurant in Brown Thomas. He used to pass the Commissionaire at its doors with awe and wonder, never looking right or left as he had been instructed, but would go immediately up to the Restaurant, wait for the lady to call him and, having accomplished his delivery, go straight out.

After some years in Copenhagen he came back to Dublin and was interviewed by Miss McGoey, the Personnel Manager at Brown Thomas. Miss McGoey told him that it was a "high-profile store", that courtesy to customers was most important and then Larry was given a job in the Food Hall as a Bacon Hand. He was now part of the store he had considered so exclusive and intimidating.

Before the foodie culture properly arrived in Dublin in the '80s, all cheeses and pâtés came from French dairy farmers. Exotic comestibles came from Fortnum and Mason. Jimmy O'Raw swears he once saw alligator's feet there! At Christmas there was a huge trade in champagnes and wines.

Chauffeur-driven cars were still a common enough sight on Grafton Street until the '80s. Lady Tiger Cowley, Indian beads in her dark plaited hair, would draw up in her chauffeured green Rolls Royce. Lady Boyd Rochfort was another. The Countess of Rosse, mother-in-law of Princess Margaret, who made her own clothes, was much seen in both shops and greatly admired. Lord and Lady Beit used to buy their provisions in the Food Hall to be collected by Albert, the chauffeur, and Mary, the Cook.

Left: *"Everything from alligator's feet to champagnes and fancy salamis".*
Opposite: *"Uh oh, watch out, its Mr Hickey again!"*

Every week Brown Thomas despatched six bottles of Blue Grass perfume to the châtelaine of a Castle in the Midlands. They were required for her bath. There was a gentleman who had a disconcerting habit of alighting from his car in his dressing-gown or emerging from the dressing-room untrousered.

Staff had its own eccentrics too. There used to be a cleaning lady who, despairing of what she saw as gullible customers as she hoovered around them, considered it her duty to inform them they could get the same item in Dunnes for half the price. A member of the Legion of Mary rounded up juniors for Retreats and threatened the pain of hellfire if they did not attend. Mr Hickey, who had not used his presentation cigarette box as it had been hoped, was still a bachelor and a director of Brown Thomas until his death in 1973. He lived in the United Services Club and disliked children so much that a child at loose around Brown Thomas was always in danger of a swipe from his walking-stick.

There were customers who regularly spent thousands in one visit. The very best were offered a reviving glass of champagne on arrival.

Switzers' customers of long-standing "were petted", in the words of Miss Hamilton Reid. If you did not hire a chauffeur, your purchases would be despatched to the porters for expert parceling and carried to the Hibernian or Shelbourne Hotels for collection. At Brown Thomas, an elegant woman would never be seen walking out of the store carrying her shopping-bags.

Store manager, Jimmy Duffy, a sprucely-dressed Scotsman in a bow-tie, was noted for his kindness to both customers and staff. Jimmy, who was there through the '80s knew all his customers. Cecily McMenamin, now running the exclusive designer-dress gallery, Private Lives, was always grateful to him for his habit of running upstairs to tell her when a regular customer of hers was on her way.

An elderly lady came into the Food Hall one day and was greeted by Jimmy Duffy. She was rather intimidated because, as she told him, she had never been in Brown Thomas before. Mr Duffy made sure her visit was a pleasant one.

A homeless man discovered half-dead in a cardboard box in Duke Lane was another recipient of Mr Duffy's kindness. Hot tea was sent out to him and Larry Yourell was commandeered to take him to the Iveagh Hostel where Mr Duffy paid for his stay.

Top: *Jimmy Duffy.*
Right: *August 1983, Galen Weston presents the first prize, a citroen car sponsored by Brown Thomas, to the best dressed lady at the Royal Dublin Society Horse Show, Mary Macdonald. One day later, tragic circumstances were avoided when armed paramilitary raiders were intercepted by a combined team of Irish soldiers and Garda at the Weston Estate in Roundwood, Co.Wicklow.*

Galen Weston, when he acquired a new property, had always considered his role to be that of providing an initial impetus and drive. Then, leaving it in the hands of committed management, he moved on to new pastures. When the Westons moved to Canada in the early '80s, George McCullagh became its Managing Director.

Mr McCullagh maintained the long established ambience of elegance and cordial relations with staff and customers. At Christmas staff parties in Brown's Restaurant, George provided the drinks. He was a racing-man and events took on an equine character. When the Phoenix Park racecourse re-opened, Brown Thomas sponsored the Brown Thomas Race and staff and customers were feted in the Brown Thomas tent, one of the first in the field of hospitality tents at social occasions. Brown Thomas sponsored the popular Best Dressed Lady competition at the Dublin Horse Show.

Brown Thomas, at the centre of Dublin and leader among the city's businesses, considered that it should be a leader in supporting social events, social causes and the city's cultural and social institutions between the Canals. The National Gallery, IMMA, the Rotunda Hospital and Dublin City University have been among the beneficiaries of its Fashion Shows and fashionable Fund Raising Balls. So have the Elderly and the Lord Mayor's Ball.

The word "Designer" achieved a new status in the 1980s. Cecily McMenamin in Private Lives, Phillip Fitzpatrick in the Men's Department ensured Brown Thomas was at the forefront of the new wave. A new gallery, Wardrobe, run by Colette Murray, supplied the young style-conscious – from the mildly cool to the fashion victim – with the hippest designer gear and gave essential encouragement and floor space to new Irish designers like John Rocha, Paul Costelloe and Quin & Donnelly.

Top: *George McCullagh, Managing Director from 1980 to 1994.*
Right: *Wally Garland and Edie McCullagh present the prizes at the Brown Thomas Phoenix Park Horse Races.*

With the inexpensive designer-look fashion chain, A-Wear, spearheaded by the dynamic Paul Kelly and Deirdre Kelly, Brown Thomas supplied the young set, aspiring to be fashionable but budget conscious. Paul Kelly would later become Managing Director of Brown Thomas when George McCullagh moved up to be Chairman of the Board.

Through the '80s, heavy staff costs and modern rationalisation as well as trends in society meant that the old ways and labour-intensive devotion to service were dying out. Wages rose but staff such as porters, seamstresses and despatch workers were inevitably shed. Switzers in 1979 had over 600 employees. By 1990 it had less than 300. Early closing on Saturdays, won in 1912, ended in the late '70s — though of course staff did not return to the six-day week.

Brown Thomas had its share of "trouble in the House" during the decade that these changes were effected. There was a strike in 1986 over the issue of late closing on certain days. In the suburbs, late closing was a fact of life. The Shop-workers Union resisted its extension to the city centre. Brown Thomas assistants brought out on strike were described as "the best-dressed picket in Dublin".

Late closing was becoming an issue that would continue into the '90s. When Brown Thomas had an "American Express" Evening for cardholders, staff refused to work. Management called in their friends and relations and everyone pitched in to make the evening a success. The right of City centre shops to open until late was upheld by the Labour Court and city assistants lost their status of, as somebody put it, "a protected species".

In 1983, Brown Thomas returned to "family ownership". The Company was removed from the Stock Market and taken on by Galen and Hilary Weston as their personal holding.

Above: *Hilary Weston*.
Opposite Top: *Paul Kelly*.
Opposite Bottom: *Deirdre Kelly*.

At this time, Dublin had four great Department stores remaining from the beginning of the phenomenon in the 1840s - Clerys, Arnotts, Switzers and Brown Thomas. Brown Thomas and Switzers were among the few of the many well-loved establishments to have proudly survived on Grafton Street. They each had had individual identities, characterised by Dublin wits as "Clerys for the Yobs, Arnotts for the Dubs, Switzers for the Prods and Brown Thomas for the Snobs…"

By now, all these demarcations between shoppers had vanished. On Grafton Street, the two great stores facing each other and enjoying the patronage of the same Grafton Street shopper still retained however a sense of competitiveness. Staff from one store rarely entered the portals of the other. Brown Thomas believed it had an edge over Switzers for elegance and glamour. Switzers referred patronisingly to Brown Thomas as "the Doll's House".

There was a sensation when, in 1991, the Switzers Group was bought from the House of Fraser by Brown Thomas. The way was laid for an even greater sensation two years later when it was announced that the two shops on Grafton Street were to merge. The old Brown Thomas building would be acquired by Marks & Spencer and, through Brown Thomas's move across the street, Switzers would be absorbed.

Dubliners, devoted fashionable shoppers and traditionalists alike, were shocked at first. But soon the good sense in the proposal became apparent. Switzers and Brown Thomas after all had always been committed to change and progress. It was one of the secrets of their success and staying-power for a century and a half.

Above: *Icons of the past.*

The reconstructed Brown Thomas, with a floor area of 140,000 sq. ft., would be much bigger than either shop had been. It would be the best of both worlds. Exclusive as the old Brown Thomas, it would also be vastly more inclusive. Those who, like Miss Hamilton Reid, regretted the disappearance of the Switzer name, could see it still, re-burnished and newly revealed over the Wicklow Street entrance.

Hilary Weston, who as Vice-Chairman of the Holt Renfrew chain in Canada (another acquisition of the Weston Group), had overseen the chain's refurbishment, was the guiding light at the new Brown Thomas.

"It will be the best department store in Europe", she had promised. Who could take issue with that? Comparable to the great stores of Paris, Tokyo and New York, it was given a uniquely Irish flavour.

Ancient Celtic motifs were given new life. And every detail, from the Ogham script carved into the stairwell to the individually cast bannisters of the graceful staircase were hand-crafted. Each yard of the hand-woven stair-carpet took five days to complete. In the Men's Department, Irish stone mosaic flooring was inspired by the landscape of the Burren. Subtle colours everywhere were given vitality with exuberant dashes of red, the familiar Brown Thomas trademark colour.

The promise was fulfilled. When the new Brown Thomas store opened for business in February 1995, it was revealed to be a fine standard-bearer for shops and shopping in the new millennium.

Top: *Chairman George McCullagh and Managing Director Paul Kelly, Design Co-ordinator Bill Simpson and Project Manager John Kielty take a lofty look at the "Construction".*
Right: *Directors Cecily McMenamin and Phil Fitzpatrick sign over the old Brown Thomas premises to Marks & Spencers.*